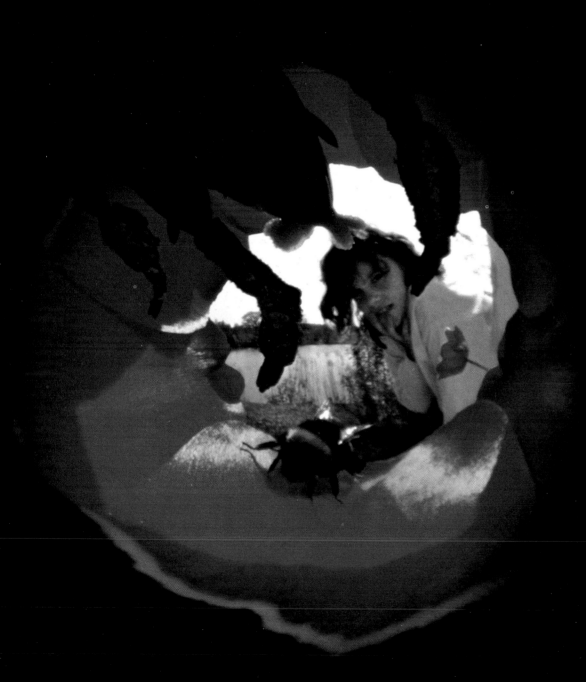

LENNART NILSSON
CLOSE TO NATURE

An Exploration of Nature's Microcosm

with
Christine Dahl   Eva Kronestedt   Nils Nykvist
Annie Skarby   Berndt Ödarp

Text by
Hans Krook

Pantheon Books
New York

 Published in the United States by Pantheon Books, a division of Random House, Inc., New York, and simultaneously in Canada by Random House of Canada Limited, Toronto.

Originally published in Sweden as *Nära Naturen* by Bonnier Fakta Bokförlag

Library of Congress Cataloging in Publication Data

Nilsson, Lennart, 1922–
Close to nature.
Translation of: Nära naturen.
1. Natural history – Pictorial works. I. Title.
QH46.N4713 1984 574′.022′2 84-7645
ISBN 0-394-54089-1

Printed and bound in Italy by Officine Grafiche A. Mondadori Editore, Verona

First American Edition

The front endpapers: *The world from inside a tulip – an example of Lennart Nilsson's special-effects photography.*

The frontispiece: *A woodland floor is rich in plant and animal life. Every time you put your foot down, you are stepping on thousands of minute organisms.*

The back endpapers: *A rhinoceros beetle* Oryctes nasicornis *and a wood ant* Formica rufa *among pine needles.*

In order to enhance the clarity of some photographs taken at very high magnifications with the scanning electron microscope, colour has been added artificially, using a special technique developed by Gillis Häägg. This applies to the following pictures: pp. 35, 39, 42, 52, 53, 54, 57, 58, 59, 60, and 61.

Contents

8
The Hidden World

10
Bees and Flowers
with Dr Eva Kronestedt and Berndt Ödarp

30
Decay and Renewal
with Professor Nils Nykvist

50
Fossil Flowers
with Annie Skarby

62
The Mosquito
with Professor Christine Dahl and Berndt Ödarp

76
Nature Under the Microscope

The Hidden World

Throughout most of history, man has looked at the natural world as a single, harmonious entity. Only in the recent past, with the development of science, has he begun to examine it more closely and pick out details in the form of orders, species, and individuals. Any of us can become familiar with a particular habitat if we are prepared to study it closely enough and learn to recognize all the plants and animals that live there. Such close contact with nature may indeed make us feel that we are an inseparable part of all the living things around us.

Yet we deceive ourselves if we think that this does more than scratch the surface of life. We know quite well that all around us is another kind of reality beyond the limited reach of our senses. The naked eye sees none of nature's more delicate structures, no micro-organisms, no glimpse of the interior of a cell, and none of the exquisite wealth of detail that adorns all living things. Natural phenomena are hidden from us in many ways. They may be too small to be seen or, for example, they may be concealed underground. Just as importantly, they may be quite ordinary, everyday things that escape our attention until someone points them out.

The development of the microscope has given us an opportunity to make contact with the hidden world of nature. Yet at first the microscope will probably tell us as little as a glance into a kaleidoscope. What we see may look beautiful and intriguing, but it is also completely incomprehensible. We have discoverd an entirely new world.

Though microscopes have been in use for about three hundred years, interpretations of what they reveal are considerably more recent. When a curious amateur constructed the first microscope he could not possibly have understood what he saw. He had no body of knowledge to help him and no reference books to turn to. No one had ever seen what the new lens revealed. Fifty years ago the scanning electron microscope opened up yet another new world, this time smaller by a factor of hundreds than anything seen before – a discovery that made the world seem even richer and more complex. Gradually, however, the structure of nature's hidden world has begun to emerge.

For instance, the microscope has shown us that virtually all living things are composed of cells, even though we cannot see them with the naked eye. All cells are astonishingly alike in structure, but each has a life of its own and in that sense a kind of individuality. They can combine to produce organisms that appear to have almost nothing in common with one another – a giraffe or an earthworm, a haddock or an ostrich, a cactus or a pear tree, a bunch of seaweed or a mushroom. We now know that cells are able to do this by co-operating with one another under the direction of their genetic material, but on its own, and to the inexperienced, a single cell from a giraffe or a brown alga would give few clues to the kind of organism it came from. We would need a lot of background information in order to identify it, and similarly our knowledge of the microworld has been pieced together from many years of research.

It is difficult to imagine how small the microworld really is. The idea is so hard to grasp that we cannot think of it directly, but instead imagine, for instance, the millions of cells together that make up a plant or even a human body. But if we wish to understand the microworld, we must rely on the evidence of our senses alone. Compared to the greater part of the animal kingdom, however, they are hardly impressive. Our senses of taste and smell are rudimentary and our hearing is feeble. Our forte is our sight, but even at close quarters we cannot discern objects less than half a millimetre or so long. We may like to think we are aware of all that goes on around us, but we perceive only a fraction of it.

The insights into the nature of reality given us by the microscope have thus revolutionized our view of the world. Even without the electron microscope, scientists had been able to form a reasonable idea of what the structure of life might be like, but what they were eventually able to see exceeded their wildest expectations. There is a vast difference between scientific theories of life and life itself in all its richness and unpredictability – as the following pages reveal. Unlike a glimpse through a microscope, however, Lennart Nilsson's photographs capture an image from the microscopic world and, by preserving it, allow us to appreciate the astonishing variety of life on earth.

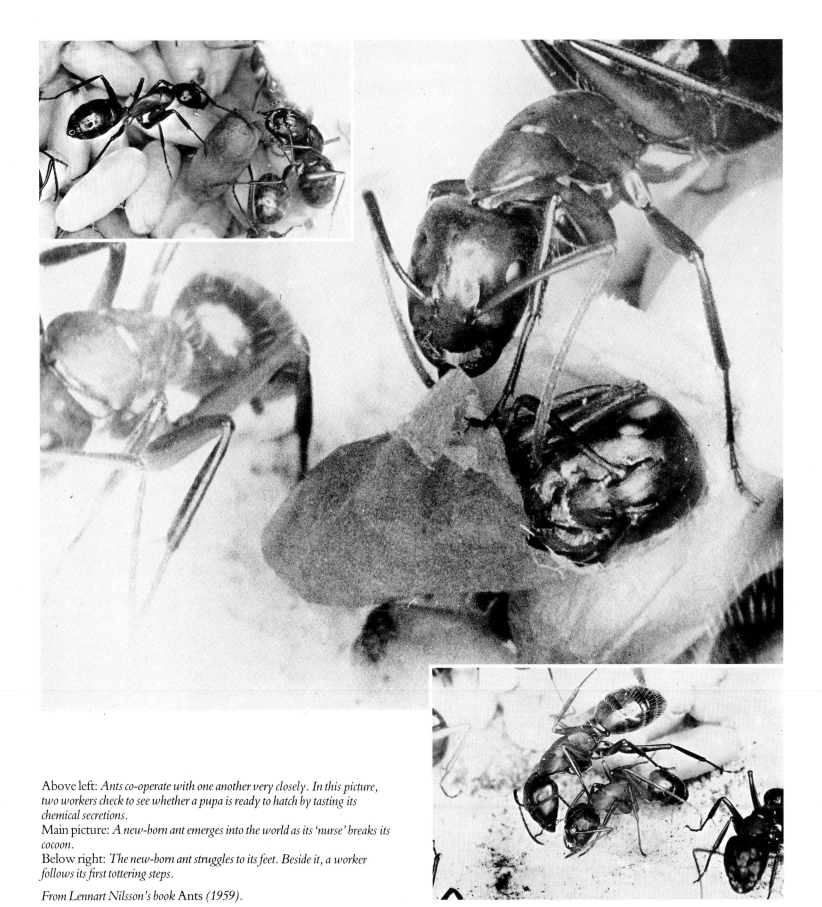

Above left: *Ants co-operate with one another very closely. In this picture, two workers check to see whether a pupa is ready to hatch by tasting its chemical secretions.*
Main picture: *A new-born ant emerges into the world as its 'nurse' breaks its cocoon.*
Below right: *The new-born ant struggles to its feet. Beside it, a worker follows its first tottering steps.*

From Lennart Nilsson's book Ants *(1959).*

Bees and Flowers

A glance at any evolutionary family tree will show that insects and man are less closely related to each other than to any other animals. Man is much more closely related to fishes and frogs, and perhaps even to starfish. It is easier to demonstrate our common ancestry with jellyfish or cuttlefish than with insects.

The insect kingdom is astonishingly diverse, partly because insects have successfully colonized virtually every corner of the earth – only the oceans have so far largely defeated them. Many insects are harmful to humans, but efforts to eradicate them have been mostly in vain. As Bertrand Russell pointed out, if insects and man were ever to confront each other, then the result would almost certainly be victory to the insects.

Even though our evolutionary links with insects are exceedingly remote, we still have much in common with some of them, particularly in terms of behaviour. Among the order of insects known as the Hymenoptera, for example, and especially the bees, we find striking abilities to communicate and organize socially. Many animals can probably communicate more successfully than we presently realize, but the ability of bees to do so to a high degree has long been known. The social communities of bees (and of some of their relatives, such as termites) show a sophistication that is almost unparalleled in the animal kingdom – with the exception of man.

A third similarity between men and bees is that the honey bee *Apis mellifera* is largely unknown in the wild. Man has cultivated seed plants and kept vertebrates as pets and domestic livestock for several thousand years, but the only spore-bearing organisms (plants that reproduce by means of tiny wind-blown spores rather than seeds) in cultivation are ferns, yeasts, and various edible mushrooms, and the only invertebrates to have been 'domesticated' are the leech, the silkworm, and the honey bee. Of these, yeasts and the honey bee are now known essentially in their cultivated forms. This makes the honey bee – apart from the silkworm – the only insect to have been domesticated. The relationship between man and bee is therefore something of a paradox: so near, and yet so far.

A bee community is composed of three castes: a queen, a mass of workers, and a smaller number of drones. The queen devotes herself entirely to reproduction and does nothing but lay eggs. The workers gather pollen and nectar from flowers. The sole purpose of the drones (who are all male) is to mate with the queen and ensure fertile eggs. Their tongues are too short to gather pollen, and to survive they depend on the pollen and nectar brought back to the hive by the workers.

As providers of honey for thousands of years, bees live in mute but close co-operation with man, but their relationship with flowering plants is even more important. Without the help of the bee many plants would be unable to pollinate one another, or at least much less easily, and without the nectar and pollen produced by plants bees would be unable to make honey. Hymenoptera pollinate more kinds of flowers than all the other insect groups combined, and bees are by far the most important members of the order. A fascinating series of adaptations in both bee and flower has made this state of affairs possible – indeed, essential.

'The birds and the bees' is a familiar cliché, but it still expresses a more poetic view of sexual life than the technical terms and blunt everyday language in which we explain the biology of reproduction. The phrase has long been used to introduce children to the supposedly delicate mysteries of sexual life, and the activities of bees among flowers in springtime is a traditional metaphor for fertility, beauty, and love, and for the relationship between them.

A noted entomologist once said that the honey bee is the only insect that we know anything about. He was alluding to the great wealth of literature on the life of the honey bee and especially to the work of Karl von Frisch, one of the founders of the study of animal behaviour. Von Frisch discovered the meaning of the honey bee's ritual 'dance', by which workers communicate to one another the whereabouts of nectar-rich flowers. At the same time, the statement makes us realize how little we still know about this largest of all animal groups.

The opposite page shows a honey bee *Apis mellifera* visiting a wood cranesbill or sticky geranium *Geranium sylvaticum*. The plant is an uncultivated member of the geranium family.

The Bee's Eye

A bee's large compound eye (above) is made up of a large number of separate optical elements called ommatidia, which vary in number according to the type of individual: a queen usually has about 3000–4000 in each eye, a worker around 5000–6000, and a drone 8000–12 000. This mass of individual elements does not, however, allow bees to focus very sharply, and bees are also insensitive to the colour red. On the other hand, they can detect both ultra-violet and polarized light, which humans cannot. Each ommatidium receives a separate image of a flower (far left), which the bee then combines to form a single picture (near left). What it actually sees, however, remains unknown, for the visual impressions are assembled by the central nervous system rather than the eye itself.

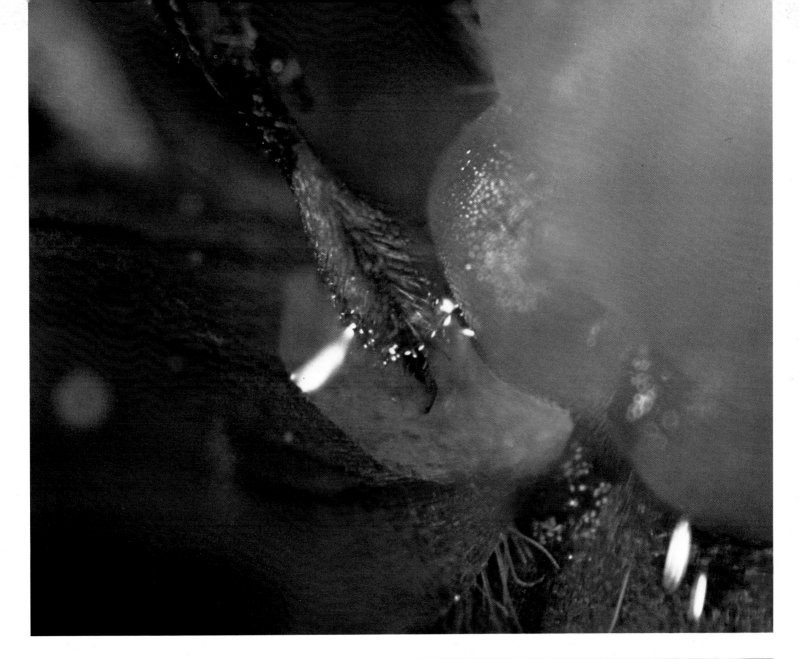

Gathering Nectar

From the age of twenty-one days onwards, the worker bee ventures out of the hive to forage for nectar and pollen. Because nectar is liquid and is often stored in inaccessible parts of the flower, bees have evolved special mouthparts to enable them to collect it. Their upper jaws are primarily designed for biting and are used in the production of honeycomb in the hive. But parts of the lower jaws have fused together into a hollow tube, surrounding an elongated tongue or proboscis, which can suck up nectar and water. The proboscis is equipped with sensors which enable the bee to assess the sugar content of the nectar.

In the picture below right, a bee's proboscis is shown searching for nectar between a flower's petals. The stamens form a tight crown and the petals are hairy at the base, enabling the nectar (which has been secreted elsewhere in the flower) to collect there. In the picture above, magnified to an even greater degree, drops of nectar can be seen among the sepals. The picture opposite shows how a bee is quickly showered with pollen in its search for nectar.

15

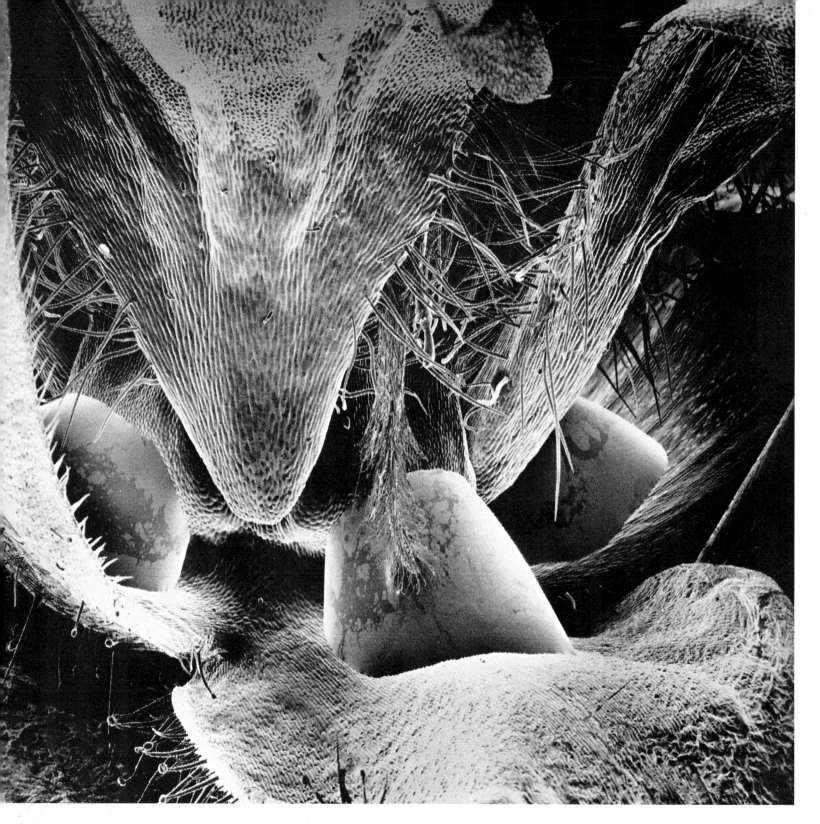

Extracting Nectar with the Tip of the Tongue

The two pictures shown here were taken with the scanning electron microscope. A bee has taste organs in its mouth, on its antennae, and on its front legs. Ten times more sensitive to sweetness than human taste buds, these organs enable the bee to concentrate on nectar with the highest sugar content, thereby minimizing its expenditure of energy in the search for food. In fact their sense of taste is so well developed that bees can distinguish between natural and artificial sugar (such as saccharin), which does not attract them.

These pictures show how a bee collects nectar. Three droplets are visible in the picture above, together with the bee's hairy, fringed tongue. The picture opposite shows a droplet changing shape as the bee begins to suck it in.

The Male Organs of a Flower

The flower is the plant's organ for fertilization and reproduction. Many plants reproduce vegetatively by, for instance, sending out runners from the parent plant, but they cannot then benefit from cross-fertilization, in which male sex cells in a pollen grain of one plant are combined with a female egg in the ovary of another. Through cross-fertilization, the variability of a species's genetic endowment is continually renewed.

The first step in cross-fertilization is the transfer of pollen from a stamen (male organ) in one flower to a pistil (female organ) in another. Many kinds of insects, including bees, perform this first step and help myriads of plants to pollinate one another. Fertilization itself takes place later, in the ovary of the female flower.

At some time in the past, insects must have discovered accidentally that nectar and pollen grains are extremely nourishing. Both plants and insects have since evolved ways of collaborating as closely as possible to make this discovery beneficial to them both.

1 *A honey bee on a wood cranesbill with pollen grains adhering to its head.*
2 *Pollen grains pour out of an anther.*
3 *The anthers of the wood cranesbill ripen in sequence: in this picture the ones at the back, forming part of an inner crown of stamens, are ripe, while those in the foreground, from the outer crown, are not yet ripe.*
4 *Both crowns of stamens are now ripe and heavily laden with pollen.*

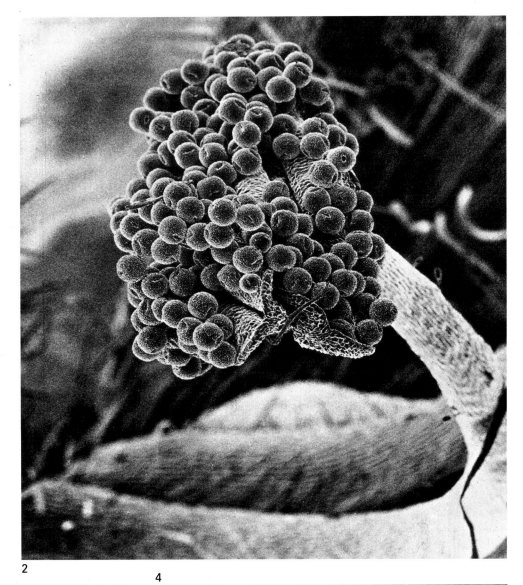

2

3

4

1

Gathering Pollen

Pollen consists of small grains produced by a flower's anthers. Each grain contains sex cells which, when fused with an egg, will lead to the creation of a new plant. In plants favoured by bees, the grains are usually prickly and coated with fatty substances so that they are easily caught up by the bee when it visits a flower. Pollen grains contain protein, fats, and carbohydrates, as well as vitamins and minerals, and are a nourishing source of food for many animals apart from bees.

Some plants generate vast amounts of pollen, but produce no nectar – roses, tulips, and poppies are typical examples. For bees, however, the real attraction of a flower lies in its sugar-rich nectar, and the purpose of nectar is precisely to entice unsuspecting insects to the flower. They can then be covered in pollen as they seek out the 'bait'.

When the upper parts of a flower's stamens, the anthers, become ripe they open and release their pollen, which pours out. In many plants, the anthers open at certain times of the day and

close within minutes or hours. Bees are apparently able to memorize this schedule and so come to the flower at exactly the right moment.

As soon as a bee alights on a flower and brushes against an anther it is showered with pollen. Being sticky and prickly, the pollen fastens on the bee's hairs. The bee may eat some of the pollen, but will gather most of it with its jaws and forelegs in order to carry it back to the hive in a pollen basket on each back leg. These baskets are formed by a double row of stiff hairs along a concave section of the lower leg. The bees habitually moisten the pollen with saliva, which contains a preservative substance.

1 *A bee need only brush against a stamen for large amounts of pollen to stick to its hairy legs.*
2 *The larger picture shows how a bee's leg literally combs the pollen grains from the anthers. In the smaller picture, the grains can be seen arranged between the rows of hairs on the bee's leg.*

Recognizing Flowers

Bees learn to recognize particular kinds of flowers by a combination of appearance and scent. They are constant in their preference and will return to the same species as long as it continues to produce pollen and nectar. This is an advantage to the flower because it ensures that the flower is pollinated by the same species. The bees benefit by being able to exploit a guaranteed supply of nectar. On returning to the hive, a scout-bee can tell its fellow workers both the distance and direction of nectar-rich flowers by performing a remarkable 'dance'.

The amount of nectar in a single flower is minute and to gather a sufficient quantity a bee may have to visit several hundred individual flowers in the course of a journey.

1 *With the pollen basket on each back leg fully laden, a bee prepares to return to the hive.*
2 *Pollen is transferred from a bee's leg to the lobes of the stigma on the pistil.*
3 *The same subject, seen under the scanning electron microscope.*

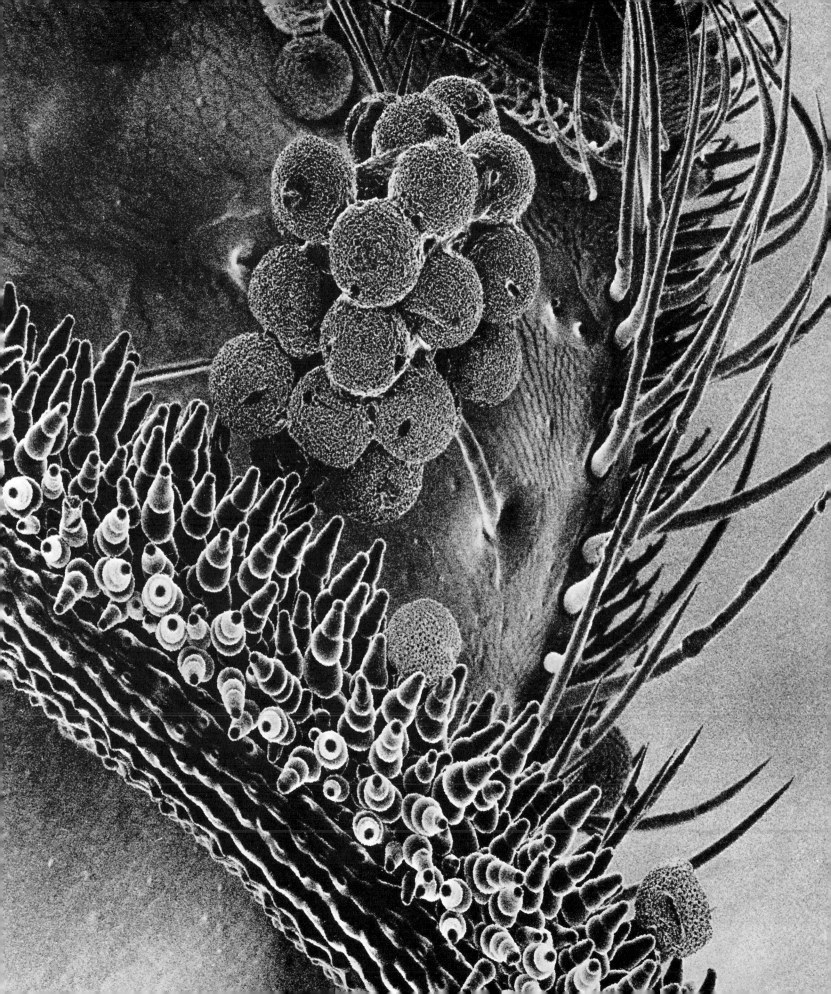

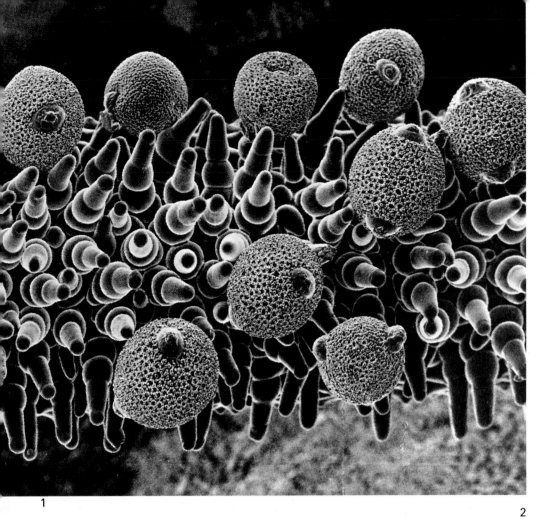

1

2

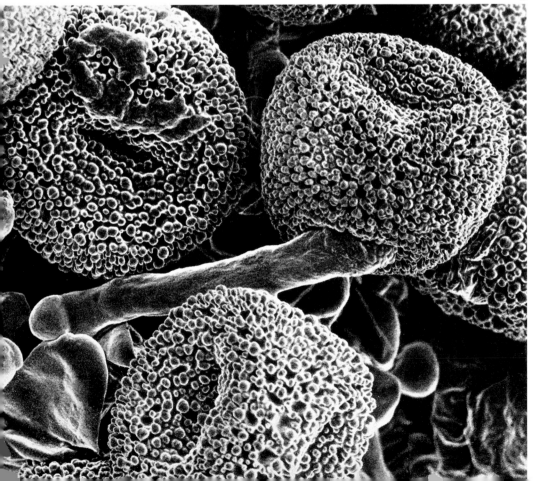

Grooming

Nectar is a sugary solution secreted by special glands called nectaries. These may be positioned almost anywhere on a flower, depending on the type of plant. Bees take some of it for their own nourishment, but the greater part is collected for the production of honey in the hive. During the search for nectar, large quantities of pollen grains stick to the bees and in this way are transferred from the stamens to the pistils of the flowers visited. Many kinds of plants visited by bees have male and female organs in separate plants. Others have them in separate flowers on the same plant, and finally some have both male and female organs in the same flower.

That this process works so well is largely due to the bee's foraging behaviour, but in part is due to its highly specialized anatomy. The bee's thorax, the middle segment of the body that connects head to abdomen, is hairy, not smooth as it is in many insects. From each hair several even finer threads, called apophyses, branch out. These act as a highly efficient trap, or net, for the collection of pollen. When a sufficient number of pollen grains have attached themselves to the hairs, the bee begins to groom itself.

The bee's grooming behaviour is very distinctive. It first combs through its head and thorax with the short, brush-like ridges of hair on its back legs, at the same time transferring any pollen on its forelegs and jaws. Having collected the pollen on its back legs, the bee then rubs them briskly together to shake the pollen into the special basket on each leg. The bee compresses the pollen in each basket with its middle legs, often in flight. When the baskets are full, the bee returns to the hive and empties them.

1 *Multitudes of tiny projections, called papillae, are shown on the part of the stigma lobes where the pollen grains have stuck* en masse. *Each papilla is composed of several cells.*
2 *Pollen grains greatly magnified. They are usually rounded in shape and their surfaces are pitted, giving the pollen of each species its characteristic appearance. In each grain's walls, openings can be seen through which a pollen tube may later grow.*
3 *Pollen grains on a bee's leg are brushed off onto the lobes of a stigma.*

3

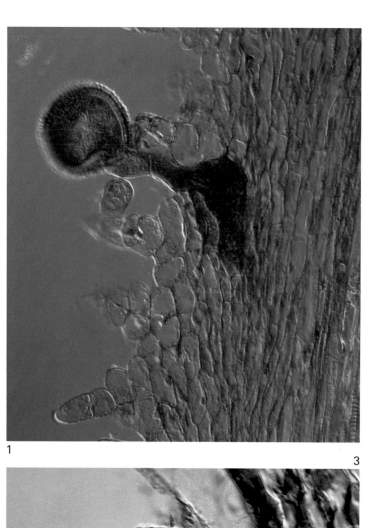

1

2

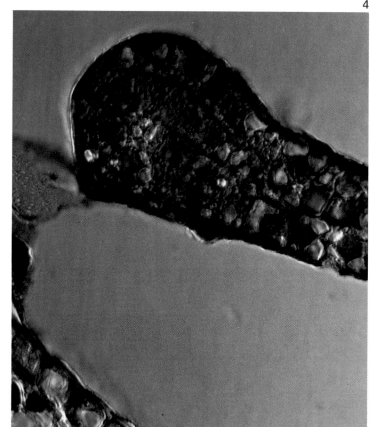

3

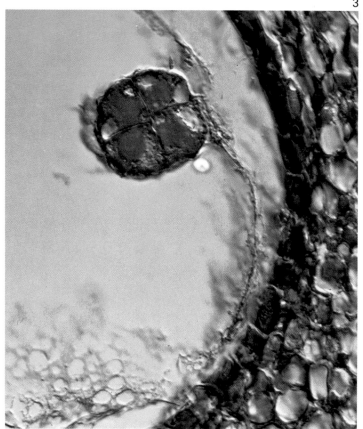

4

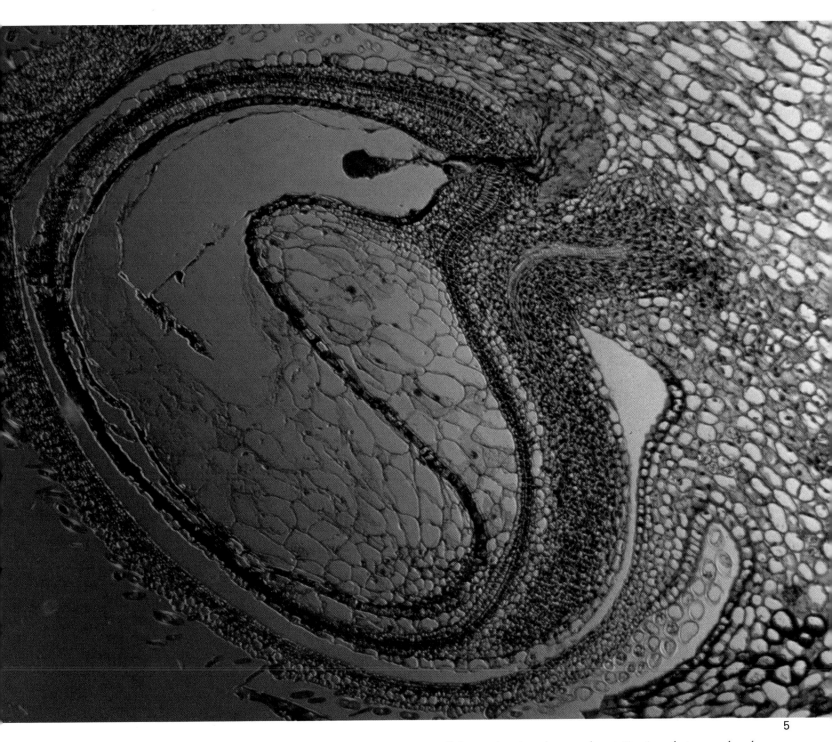

Fertilization of the Wood Cranesbill

1 *A pollen grain has attached itself to the stigma wall and its pollen tube has penetrated the stigma tissue.*

2 *Several pollen tubes growing down, in competition with one another, through the pistil tissue.*

3 *The plant embryo at an early stage, in the embryo sac. Fertilization has now taken place, meaning that a male cell nucleus in the pollen tube has fused with a female cell nucleus in the embryo sac. In fact there were two cell nuclei in the pollen tube: the other has fused with the central fusion nucleus, as it is*

called, to produce the endosperm, the nutritive tissue that surrounds and nourishes the embryo during its growth.

4 *The embryo has now undergone a number of cell divisions and has taken on a club-like shape. One can begin to discern a pattern in the arrangement of the cells and the reddish cell nuclei are also visible.*

5 *A seed that has just begun to germinate. Its early growth is fuelled by the nutritive tissues of the endosperm.*

(All five pictures were taken from slide sections prepared for optical microscopy.)

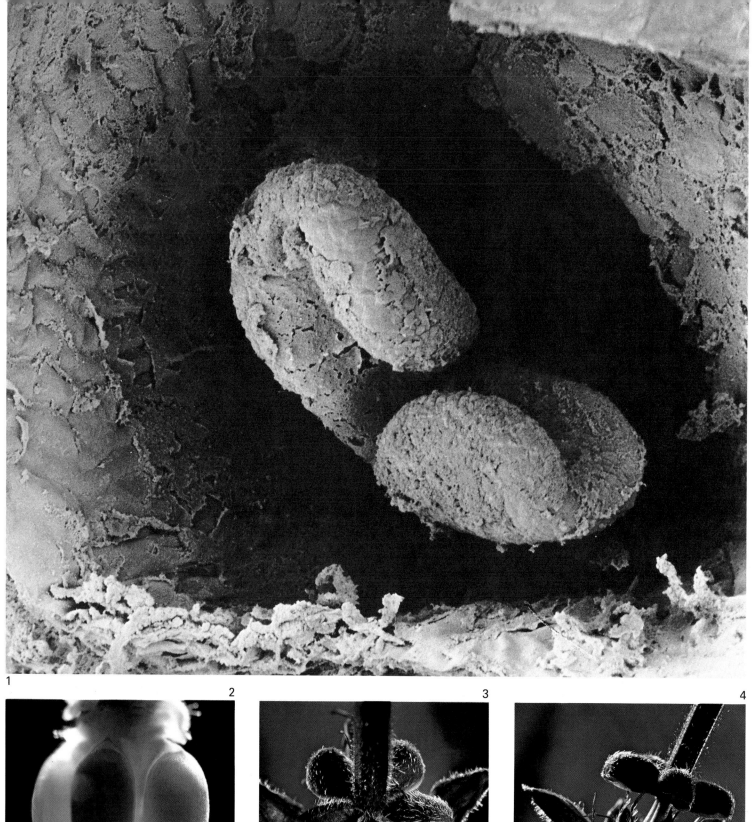

1

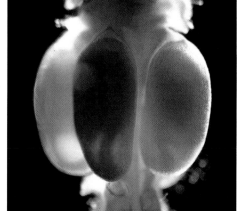

2

3

4

5

Germination

1 *The embryo opened for the photograph in order to reveal the two cotyledons.*
2 *The embryo at a later stage: the cotyledons have begun to develop.*
3 *The wood cranesbill's petals have fallen. This occurs as soon as fertilization has taken place in order to discourage foraging insects, but the sepals remain.*
4 *Seed pods may open in many different ways. Here in the wood cranesbill seeds are scattered by a sudden explosive rupture; tensions in the pod walls cause it to burst and eject the seeds with tremendous force.*
5 *The seed has now germinated and a new plant meets daylight for the first time.*

When a seed germinates, the embryo (the part of the seed that contains the cells of the new plant) has usually begun to develop and already displays the rudiments of its future parts: root, stem, and leaf. It will also bear either one or two seed-leaves, or cotyledons, which are much simpler in structure than are later maturing leaves. Most kinds of flowering plants – the wood cranesbill, for example, shown here – have two cotyledons.

Access to air, the correct temperature, and the right amount of moisture are required for the seed to germinate at all. If these requirements are met, the plant is soon able to draw nutrients from the soil and no longer depends on the seed's special food supply in the nutritive tissue (the endosperm) that originally surrounded the embryo.

Directed by growth hormones, the root of the germinating seed begins to grow downwards and the shoot pushes up into the air. The root is at first enclosed in a sheath, which it splits. It then spreads down into the soil, takes hold with its innumerable hairy outgrowths, and begins to absorb moisture and nutrients.

The plant actually grows from two points – the tip of the root and the apex of the shoot. These are present in rudimentary form in the seed. The extreme tip of the root is protected by a special cap and the apex of the shoot by young leaves. If either growing point is damaged the plant will die.

Decay and Renewal

'Earth to earth, dust to dust, ashes to ashes....' For some, the words of the Christian funeral service simply confirm the finality of death. Others, however, view them as an affirmation of man's role as a link in an eternal chain, as a small step in an endless journey along the path of life. This applies to every living thing: the grass and the cow, the lion and the gazelle – all will eventually return (in the chemical and physical sense) to the earth that brought them into existence and provide the raw material for new forms of life.

This unending cyclical pattern involves the same material compounds, the same atoms ceaselessly building molecules. Many attempts have been made to explain it in an easily understandable way. For instance, it is often said that a form of near-eternal life can be traced in the circulation of water, for the same water circulates in one way or another for millenia. From time to time some of it is absorbed in a human body, but when the person dies it returns to the earth, thence to begin another cycle. If Queen Cleopatra's water molecules were distributed evenly throughout the earth's water supply, then a single glass of tap water would contain a quarter of a million of them.

Matter is transformed in many such continuous cycles. Carbon, from carbon dioxide incorporated by plants during photosynthesis, is released by respiration or bacterial activity and returns to the atmosphere. Plants absorb nitrogen via inorganic compounds in the soil and use it to synthesize protein. When a plant dies, bacteria convert the nitrogen back to inorganic compounds which other plants can take up again. A small amount of atmospheric nitrogen is converted to a usable form by the electrical action of thunderstorms, but the vast proportion of nitrogen 'fixation' is accomplished by micro-organisms.

Nature's chemical processes may be continuous, but they proceed at varying rates. Examine a handful of soil and you will see why. At first glance, it will be found to consist of various kinds of mineral grains – quite simply, fragments of rock. But between and on the grains, you will find the remains of what were once living plants and animals. You will also find vast numbers of bacteria, as well as fungal threads, single-celled plants and animals, and many other organisms.

Decaying organic material is the most important source of nourishment for growing plants. Dead plants and animals are attacked by bacteria and fungi which gradually break them down into simple chemical compounds. In this way, the micro-organisms are able to satisfy their need for energy, while the dead organism's nutrients are made available to living plants. The complex and varying material formed by the partial breakdown of vegetable and animal matter is called humus.

Bacteria thrive in broad-leaved, or deciduous, vegetation with a neutral or basic soil. If soil aeration is good, then decaying material is easily transformed into fertile humus. This in turn encourages earthworms, which aerate and lighten the topsoil still further; their importance in soil ecology cannot be overemphasized. In coniferous woods, on the other hand, the soil is more acidic and so less suitable for bacteria, and the task of breaking down organic material falls to various kinds of fungi. They work more slowly than the bacteria of deciduous woods and decomposition proceeds only so far as the more complex chemical compounds. These cannot be absorbed so easily by the plant cover above, which depends on particular kinds of fungi to break the compounds down still further. As fungi are not particularly attractive to burrowing organisms, the organic remains tend to accumulate in a layer above the topsoil.

It is remarkable that until recently soil ecology was so little regarded. Without fertile humus, properly aerated by earthworms, few plants could obtain the nutrients they need to survive. It can best be thought of as a kind of border between the living and the dead, an intermediate stage through which animals and plants must pass before they can be converted to other forms of life. A compost heap represents the process in a shortened and highly concentrated form: what takes place is still natural, but it is artificially speeded up.

Withering autumn leaves and spring seedlings are both stages of one and the same cycle – the everlasting rotation of living things through the soil. Each point in the cycle is only a phase of apparent rest: although we may be unable to detect any changes, in the microworld changes are taking place all the time.

1

The Build-up

In photosynthesis, green plants produce the organic compounds that help them to grow by using energy absorbed by chlorophyll – a kind of pigment – from sunlight. The plants in turn provide a source of energy for all living things. The need to absorb as much sunlight as possible is what produces the layered, mosaic-like arrangement of the leaves in the crown of a tree (above) which almost block out the sky when you look up the trunk from below.

The right-hand picture shows a leaf in cross-section. The outer layer at top and bottom is the leaf's skin, or epidermis. This secretes a protective film, the cuticle, which restricts water loss. In between are long columnar cells which contain chlorophyll and are the main photosynthesizing region of the leaf. Below them on the underside of the leaf is looser, spongy tissue which, being less dense, is a paler shade of green.

1 *Foliage of the Norway maple* Acer platanoides *seen from below*.
2 *Cross-section of a leaf under the scanning electron microscope*.

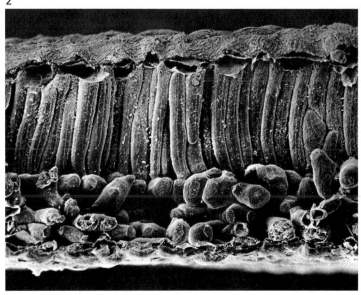

2

Autumn Leaves

As winter approaches, most trees cease to draw water from the ground, and deciduous ones shed their leaves in order to minimize water loss. This process begins several days before the leaves begin to fall, when the cells that connect the leaf-stalk to its branch break down or separate, cutting off the leaf's food supply. The pictures on the left show how a maple leaf is shed.

The network of branches on the now leafless treetops (above right) shows how evenly distributed the foliage has been in order to absorb the maximum amount of sunlight.

Leaves on the ground (below right). A leaf's usefulness is not over once it has been shed. On the ground, the decomposing action of bacteria break down its chemical compounds, leading to the release of carbon dioxide and plant nutrients which can be reabsorbed by the living vegetation.

It is a fact of life that leaves wither and turn yellow in autumn – but why? Superficially, it may seem that lower temperatures simply destroy a plant's chlorophyll, thereby causing its leaves to loosen and fall to the ground.

In fact it is not nearly so simple. Chlorophyll is destroyed in most kinds of plants in the autumn, but remains throughout the winter in others (for example, the cowberry *Vaccinium vitis-idaea* and conifers). As the chlorophyll decays, other pigments become visible, such as orange-coloured carotene and yellow xanthophyll; they have been present in the leaf all year, but until now the chlorophyll masked them. Some plants, such as copper beech, have pigments that permanently conceal the chlorophyll, and hence are never green.

Living leaves also carry several other pigments. The cytoplasm itself is colourless, but often contains water-soluble pigments called anthocyanins, which turn red in acid but blue in basic solutions. Their autumn glory is conspicuous in such plants as maple and Virginia creeper.

Finally, the cell contents shrivel away entirely and all the pigments, too, disappear. Only the leaf's veins remain, a system of tough connective tissues – a decorative skeleton, thin as gauze but remarkably strong.

The pictures on the opposite page follow the shedding of a maple leaf. First, the cells that connect the leaf stalk to its branch break down or separate, cutting off the leaf's food supply (top right). Over a short period the stalk gradually loosens and finally detaches itself (below), and the leaf tumbles to the ground (far left).

1

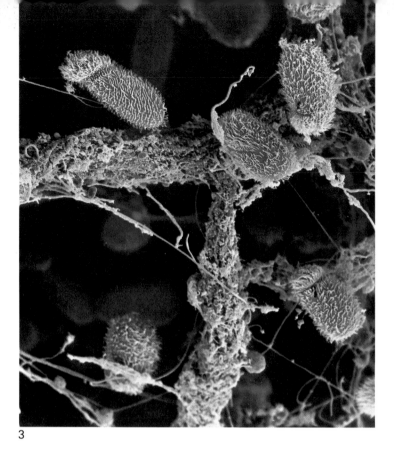

2

3

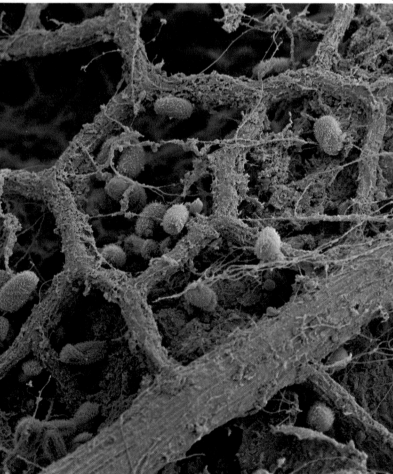

Decay

Nature wastes nothing. Everything is exploited; everything has a future use. By the following spring, most of the autumn's fallen leaves are no more than skeletons – outlines of leaf-veins. Yet even these may still contain large numbers of the bacteria that originally colonized the leaf and broke it down into simple compounds.

The leaf tissue is the first part to decay. The leaf-veins, which carried water and nutrients to the cells of the living leaf, remain as an airy lattice-work.

The pictures on this page show a maple leaf progressively enlarged. Even in the second picture, small single-celled organisms are fully visible. The top picture on the opposite page shows one of these bacteria-eating organisms in close-up, a free-living protozoan that propels itself by beating its cilia (short, thread-like growths that project from the surface of a cell), which form a kind of furry sheath around it.

1 *A decaying maple leaf, shown life-size. The living leaf's tough outer protective layer, the cuticle, has disintegrated and now the leaf's remaining interior cells are exposed to bacteria and fungi.*
2 *A close-up of the leaf's vein structure. An abundance of micro-organisms can be seen in the exposed contents of the cells. Magnified 180 times.*
3 *The same leaf-veins magnified 500 times.*
4 *A ciliate, a micro-organism which feeds on bacteria, shown full length and magnified about 1600 times. The yellow threads are probably fungal hyphae. The picture has been coloured artificially.*
5 *The tip of the ciliate's mouth. The hair-like cilia around it are mobile and sweep water and bacteria into the organism. Ciliates can survive only in water, but the thin film remaining on the decaying leaf is enough. Magnified 2500 times.*
6 *A close-up of the ciliate's mouth aperture. The small oval yellow particles are bacteria. Magnified 5300 times.*

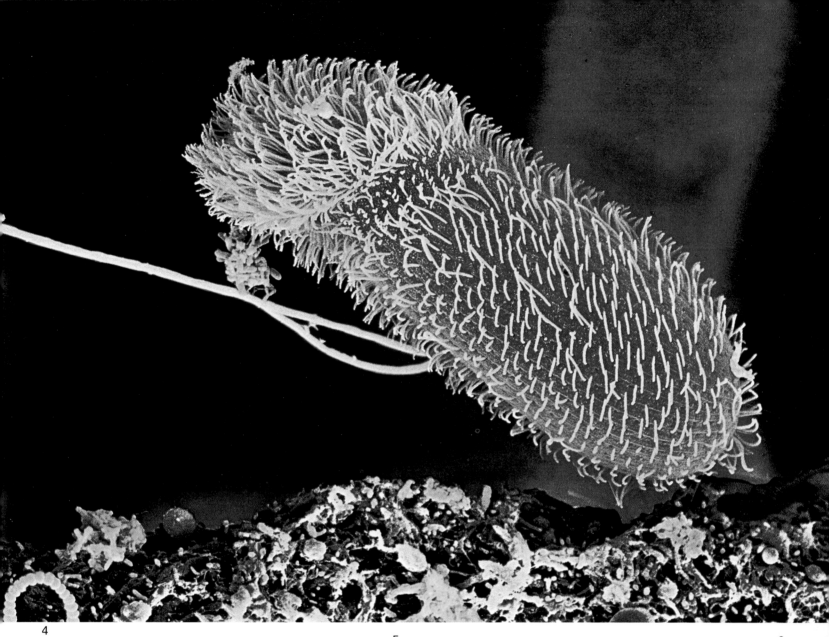

4

5

6

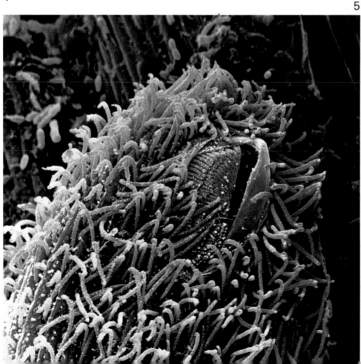

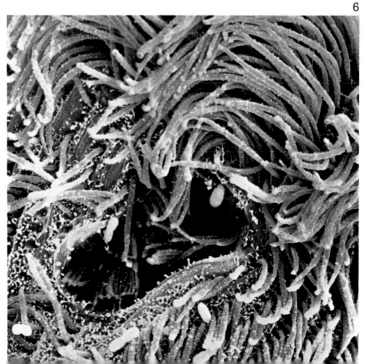

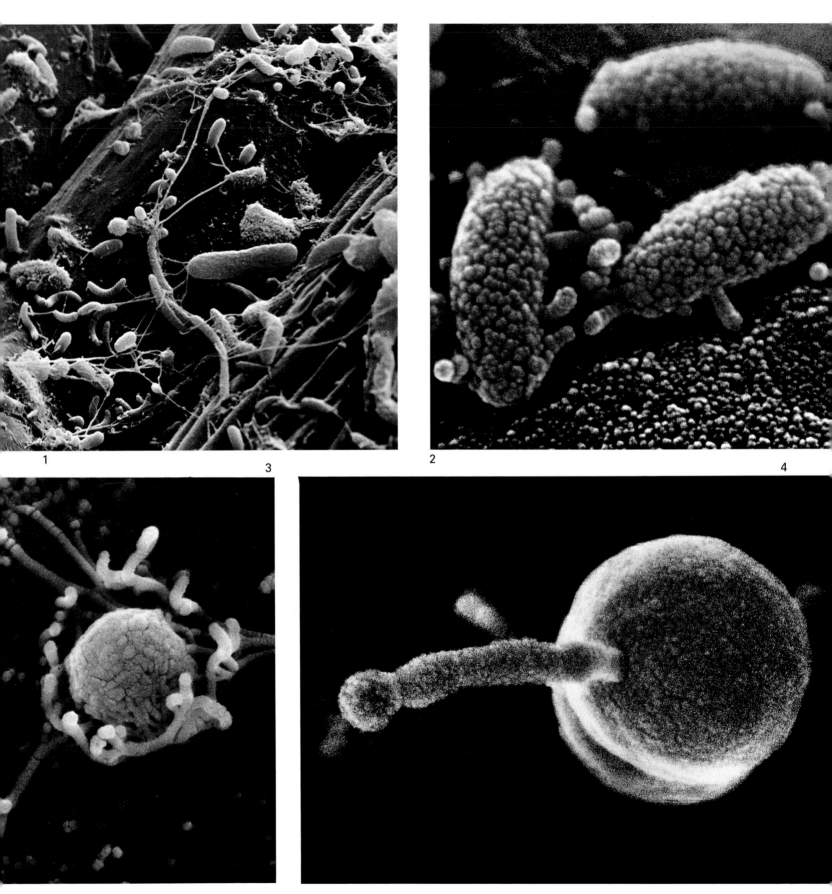

Micro-organisms

On a magnified section of a decaying maple leaf (the picture at top left on the opposite page), tiny organisms of various kinds can be seen. The thin threads are fungal hyphae (the filaments of which most fungi are composed) or baterial detritus, and the oval or rounded bodies are probably bacteria – though some may be fungal spores. The top right-hand picture on page 36 shows some micro-organisms magnified to an even greater degree.

Using the scanning electron microscope, it is now possible to study the microworld in more detail than ever before. Such advanced technology has led to the discovery of minute organisms whose existence was previously unknown. Some of these are shown in the two bottom pictures on the opposite page. They have not yet been named.

Myriads of bacteria-eating organisms flourish among the rich bacterial flora of decaying leaves. Many are virtually unknown to science, simply because hardly anyone has yet seen them. Some may be foraminiferans, relatives of the common amoeba. Some have pseudopodia, or projections of the cell, with which they propel themselves and ingest bacteria and fungal hyphae. Others have cilia or various outgrowths with which they seize their prey.

All the organisms do their utmost to extract the organic nutrients from the cells of the leaf. Bacteria consume them directly, bacteria-eating organisms indirectly. The pictures to the right give an idea of the immense variety of bacteria-eating protozoans. They will begin to appear on dead leaves after the leaves have been soaked in water for a week or so.

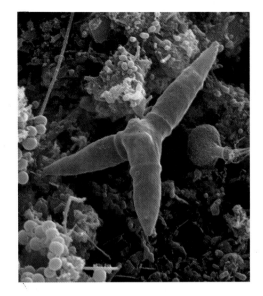

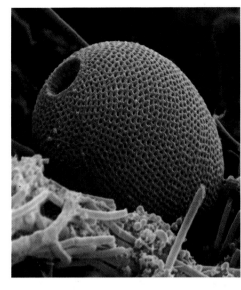

1 Part of a decaying maple leaf, magnified 5000 times. The threads are mostly fungal hyphae and the oval or rounded bodies bacteria.
2 Bacteria, magnified 75000 times.
3 An unknown micro-organism, magnified 60000 times.
4 An unknown micro-organism, magnified 170000 times.
The six pictures on the right show some of the bacteria-eating micro-organisms that develop on a decaying leaf.

1

Fungi

In acid or neutral soils, fungi are extremely important decomposing agents. They occupy a unique and peculiar place among organisms. Unlike members of the plant kingdom, with which they were formerly grouped, fungi lack chlorophyll and the cell walls of most species are not composed of cellulose but of chitin. Most fungi consist of long tubular threads, called hyphae, which commonly form an underground web, or mycelium; this can be surprisingly extensive. The hyphae penetrate plant debris and gradually displace bacteria. The latter are able to reproduce very quickly and so are the first to colonize dead leaves, but they are powerless to resist the subsequent advance of the hyphae.

Fungi reproduce asexually by means of spores at the tips of specialized hyphae. These are produced in huge numbers. Some fungi grow large fruiting bodies consisting of a compact mass of hyphae, often above ground, in which spore formation takes place. The familiar edible mushroom is a typical example. The underground network of hyphae, the mycelium, forms the 'trunk' of the fungus; this persists, while the fruiting bodies themselves are short-lived. Thus when a mushroom is picked or withers away, the mycelium remains – which is why mushrooms are to be found in the same places year after year.

In ideal conditions – on a mouldy slice of bread, for example – fungal hyphae are able to expand until they form an even, furry mat. But on a woodland floor their progress is usually restricted by various organisms that feed on the hyphae, such as microscopically small mites. The picture on the right shows a mite on a web of hyphal threads.

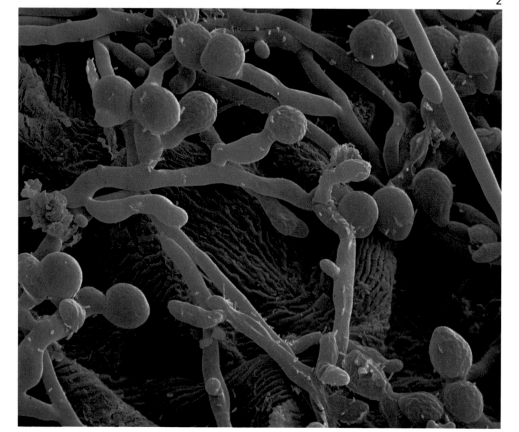

2

1 *A damp, decaying maple leaf which whitish fungal hyphae have begun to colonize.*
2 *The hyphae, with spores at their tips, magnified about 1300 times under the scanning electron microscope.*
3 *A mite on its source of nutrition, a dense mat of fungal hyphae. Magnified 90 times.*

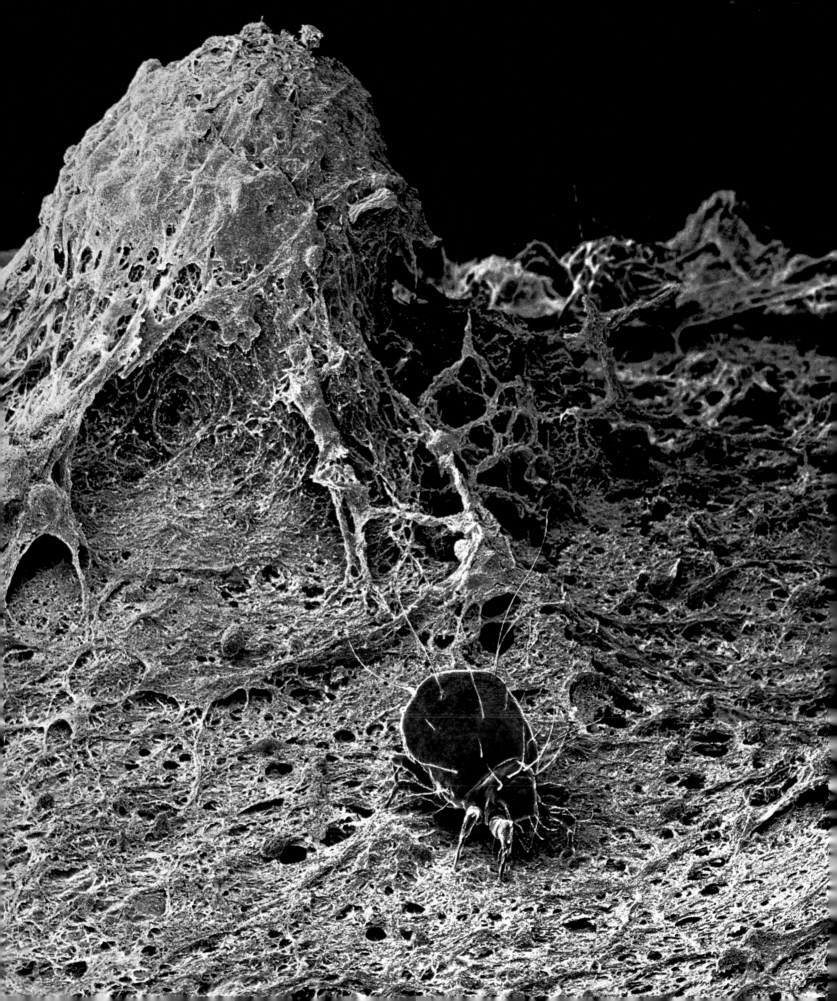

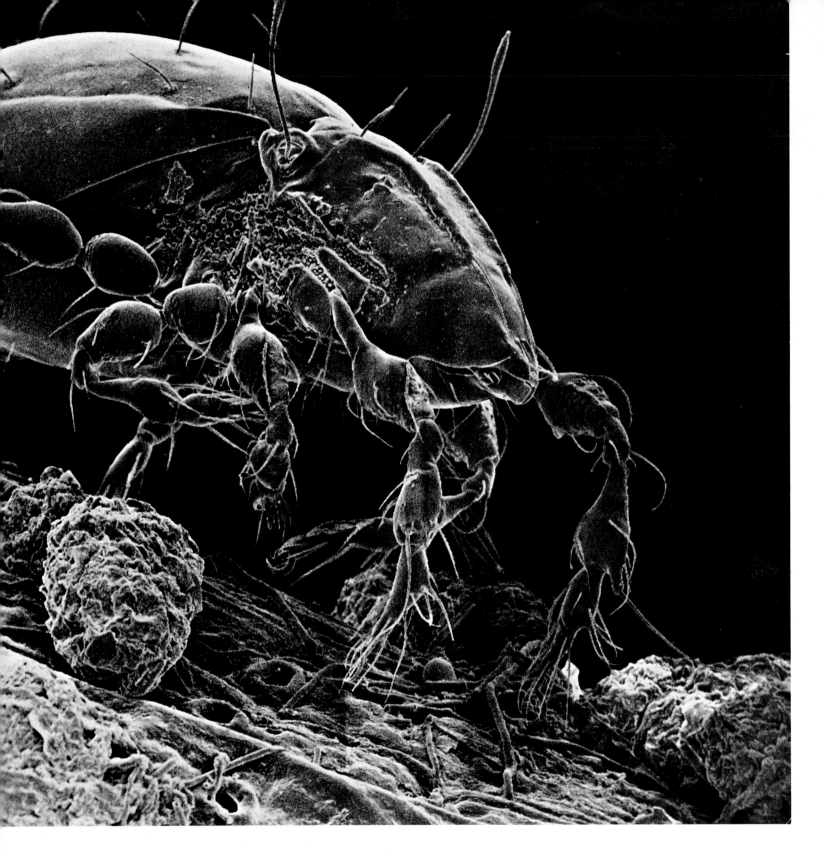

Mites

About ten thousand different species of mites have so far been identified. The most common are the various kinds of horned mite which live in the soil. The picture above shows one of them on a pine needle. It has been estimated that every time you put your foot down in a coniferous forest you are treading on about five thousand of these mites. The picture opposite shows mites of another species, mating. It was taken with the scanning electron microscope, magnified about 1600 times.

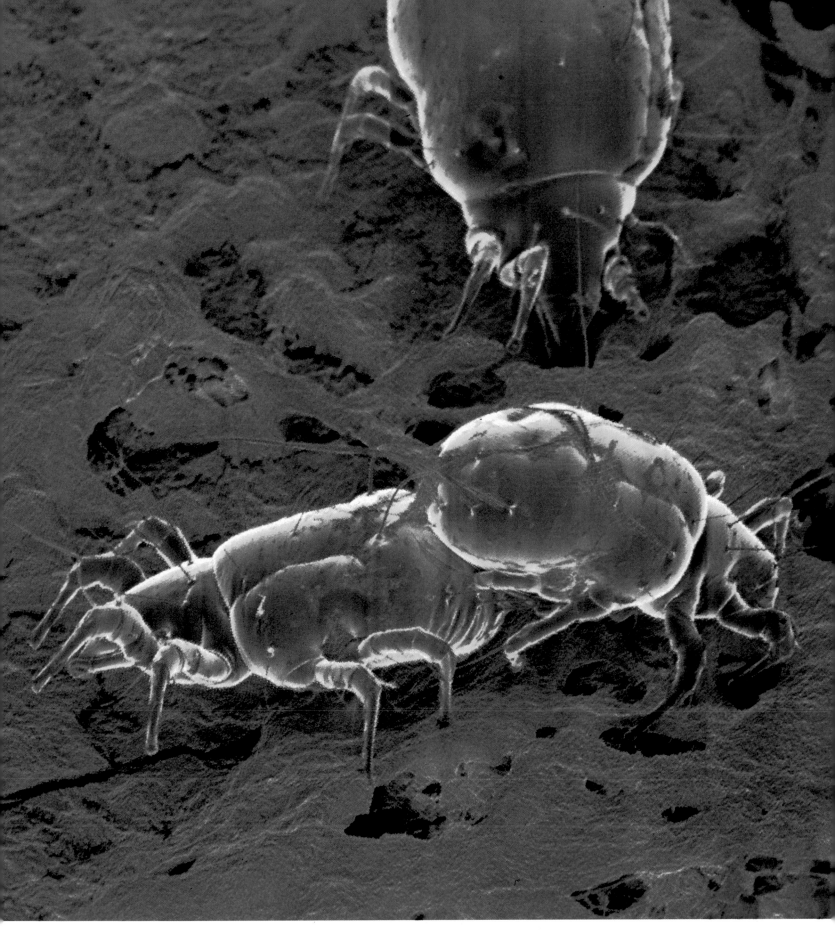

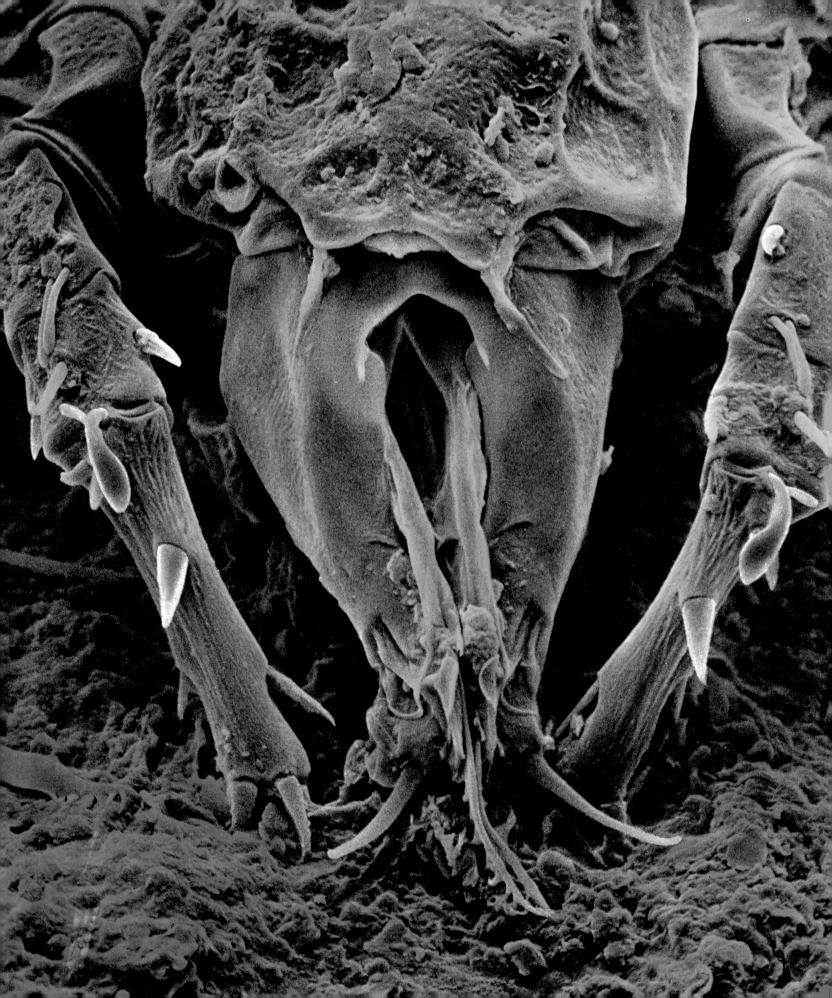

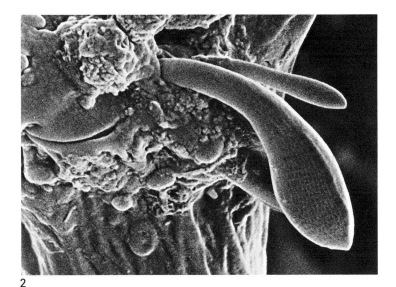

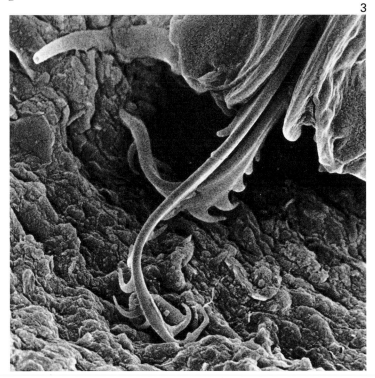

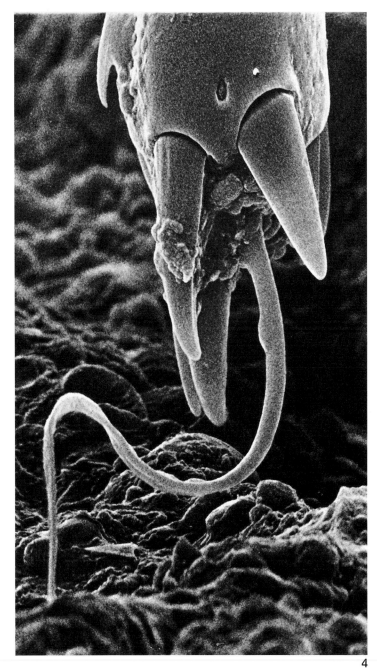

4

A Mite's Anatomy

Mites are members of the class Arachnida, which also includes spiders. They are extremely small, as a rule between a few hundredths and a tenth of a millimetre long, and can survive in almost any conditions: above ground, under stones, on dead animals and plants. Some mites live in water, both fresh and salt, while others are parasites on man and other animals, including insects such as dung-beetles and bumble-bees. Animal droppings often contain huge numbers of them.

Animals that live permanently underground are usually blind and depend on their other senses, which are well developed. They may be extremely sensitive to sound or to minute changes in the chemical composition of the soil. They must also be able to burrow effectively. A mite's foot has projections resembling hooves which enable it to move across wet, slippery surfaces. At the tip of each front leg there are highly sensitive tactile growths whose function is probably to detect the presence of chemical substances important to the mite's diet. Its 'nose' is higher up on the front legs.

1 *The forelegs and jaws of a species of mite which is particularly common in compost heaps and feeds chiefly on bacteria. The two spiny projections in the mouth opening at the centre of the picture are used to draw food into the mouth.*
2 *A detail from the large picture opposite, showing the mite's 'nose', which consists of an outgrowth on the upper part of each foreleg. Magnified 2000 times.*
3 *A detail of the mite's mouth.*
4 *The mobile sensory cilia on the mite's foot.*

1

2

3

4

44

Springtails

In addition to mites, various kinds of springtail are another important group of creatures which feed largely on fungal hyphae in the soil. The picture at the top of the opposite page shows, among other things, a blackish-brown mite in the centre with a springtail to its right. This kind lives mainly above ground and therefore has long antennae, eyes, and a well-developed forked appendage on its hind parts which enables it to 'spring' away when in danger. Springtails that live underground are blind and have a much-reduced tail appendage. Examples of these can be seen in the centre picture at the bottom of the opposite page.

Predators

The huge numbers of organisms that feed on bacteria and fungal hyphae are kept in check by various predators. The bottom left-hand picture on the opposite page shows two pseudoscorpions, less common predators than the relatively abundant predatory mites, one of which is shown in the bottom right-hand picture. The mite has caught a springtail and in the bottom right-hand picture on this page (taken with the scanning electron microscope) we see the same mite in the act of devouring its prey.

Mites display great variation in shape. The top right-hand picture on this page shows another species, with hairier, more spider-like legs.

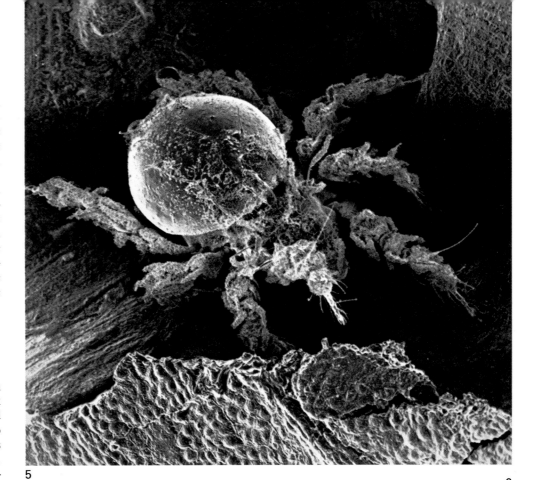

5

6

1 *A blackish-brown mite is shown in the centre of the picture, with a reddish-brown mite of another species below and to the left of it. To the right of the picture is a springtail.*
2 *Two pseudoscorpions.*
3 *Springtails beneath a web of fungal hyphae.*
4 *A mite with a springtail it has just captured.*
5 *Another species of mite under the scanning electron microscope.*
6 *A mite devouring a captured springtail. Magnified about 100 times.*

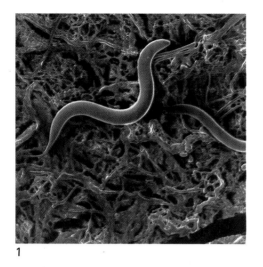

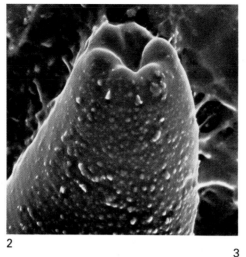

Nematodes and Fungi

Nematodes, or roundworms, are minute worms that occur in profusion in the soil. Where food is plentiful, there may be several million per square metre. There are a large number of different kinds which vary greatly in appearance, but all nematodes are basically similar in structure. They are found in almost every kind of soil and in some of the most inhospitable places on earth – in snow at both the North and South Poles, and at considerable depths in lakes and the sea. They also occur in warm cellars, where they can tolerate temperatures of up to 40° Centigrade.

The top left-hand picture shows a group of nematodes and to the right is a close-up of a nematode's mouth. Some nematodes feed on bacteria or fungal hyphae, but there are also parasitic varieties, such as hookworm, which infest the human body. Some of these are only parasitic as larvae – and therefore use the human body as a temporary host – but others are parasitic as adults, too.

A large number of species attack crops – the potato eelworm, for example – and unless controlled can cause serious damage. They are extremely difficult to eradicate, however, because they can remain dormant in sterile soil for several years, only to revive when conditions improve.

Nematodes also have enemies of their own. Apart from predatory micro-organisms, some kinds of fungi have become adept at trapping them. These fungi, which also feed on plant debris, are sensitive to chemicals secreted by the nematodes. When they detect one, they form their hyphal threads into loops in which the nematode soon becomes entrapped, shortly to be digested and absorbed.

The large centre picture to the left shows a predatory fungus's looped web, with a nematode in the process of being caught. The two pictures below narrate the subsequent course of events: the nematode becomes entangled and then shrivels up.

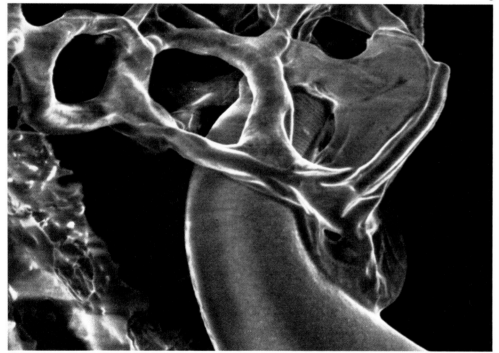

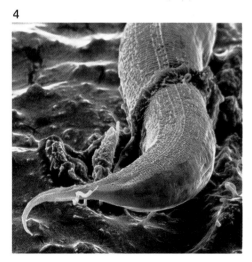

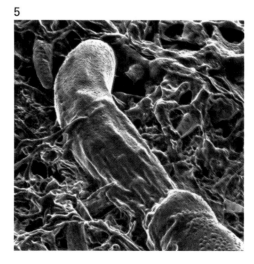

1 *Nematodes among plant debris.*
2 *A nematode's mouth under the scanning electron microscope.*
3 *A nematode becoming entangled in the looped hyphae of a predatory fungus.*
4 *The nematode is now trapped by the fungus.*
5 *The dead nematode is absorbed by the fungus.*
6 *These leaf remains, photographed from below and looking up toward the sky, are as delicate as filigree work. A red mite is sitting on the web of leaf-veins with a ground beetle below and to the left of it.*

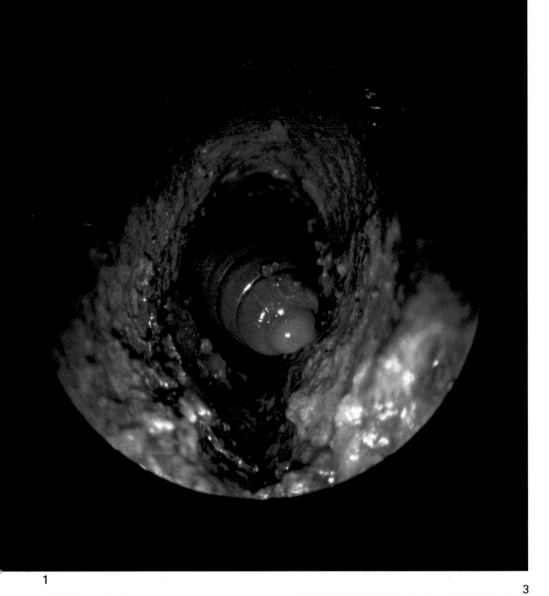

1

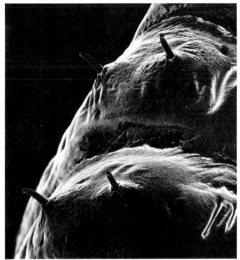

2

Soil Formation

In the final stage of the decomposition of organic material by micro-organisms all that remains are carbon dioxide, water, and in the case of plants, various substances previously absorbed from the soil. But the process of decomposition is a slow one and plant litter must pass through a large number of intermediate stages collectively termed 'humus' or plant mould. For some reason, we immediately think of death and decay when we hear the word 'mould' – but in fact it has more to do with the source and foundation of life.

Humus is of great importance to soil fertility. In a coniferous forest it mainly takes the form of a continuous layer above the topsoil, whereas in deciduous or broad-leaved woods, especially those with a high proportion of hardwood species, humus and soil become mixed together. This fertile mix, easily the richest soil for plants, is produced by the action of burrowing organisms – above all, by earthworms. Their importance to the physical health of the soil is vital.

3

1 *An earthworm entering its hole. It has dragged in a decaying leaf, which it will now devour.*
2 *The earthworm's movements through the soil are made easier by a number of bristles on each segment of skin. These act like a caterpillar's feet, or even crampons.*
3 *A pinch of soil, with sharp-edged mineral grains of various kinds, fungal hyphae, and loose humus, all of which can retain a great deal of moisture. The gaps between the soil particles allow atmospheric oxygen to filter through.*
4 *After decay, renewal. A fresh shoot pushes up through a withered maple leaf.*

4

Fossil Flowers

The history of the earth and of life itself is still largely a mystery. We can only discern the broad outlines of evolutionary development; its details have mostly not survived. Fossils, however, do provide evidence – the only kind we have – of how life may have evolved in past ages. They are mute and yet eloquent witnesses to vanished eras and we can interpret them because their evidence is more than simply representational. They reveal not only what extinct organisms may have looked liked, but how they may have lived as well. Fossils are mute only in so far as they can neither confirm nor deny the truth of what we read into them.

Our ability to make sense of the fossil record does not date back far. A little more than a century ago, the world was not considered old enough for the gradual evolution of plants and animals to have taken place. Today, evolutionary theory is the basis of all biological science. When the petrified remains of extinct organisms were first discovered, people were quite unable to estimate their age. They simply believed that fossils were evidence of the Great Flood.

The word 'fossil' means 'dug up'. But the first thought that often comes to mind is of something petrified – a living thing overwhelmed by a molten mass and hermetically sealed for future discovery. It is quite likely that such an idea stems from our knowledge of the eruption of Vesuvius in AD 79 when people and animals in Pompeii and Herculaneum were engulfed in ash and instantly fossilized.

By and large, micro-organisms completely destroy dead plants and animals, leaving only carbon dioxide, water, and an insignificant amount of mineral residue. Under the right conditions, however, all or part of a plant or animal may be preserved. Fossilization can happen in one of three ways. First, and most rarely, remains can simply dry out in the air, resulting in the mummification of softer tissues. Second, the mineral residues, again usually of softer parts, can become carbonized, leaving an impression or film of carbon on surrounding rock. This is the case with most fossil plants. Finally, the persistent hard parts of an organism can become petrified or moulded in sediments. Fossils of the third kind are the most common and often consist of compounds such as silica or calcite. They are consequently hard as stone. Alternatively, some may be embedded in amber or clay.

In the region of Lake Ivo in Skåne (the southernmost province of Sweden), china clay has long been mined for the porcelain industry. The clay, or kaolin, was formed millions of years ago by the action of alkaline water (water with a high pH value) in breaking down granite bedrock and gneiss. The particles were then carried away as silt by rivers and floods and deposited in stratified layers. In these sediments one can, with the help of a powerful microscope, detect the remains of tiny carbonized plants. Pieces of stem, leaf fragments, fruit, seeds, and even whole flowers have been discovered. Plant fossils have always been rarer than animal fossils, perhaps partly because they are less conspicuous but also because plants have no hard parts to be preserved.

1 The face of a china clay quarry at Skåne, in southern Sweden.
2 A conventional type of fossil flower, consisting of a thin film of carbon imprinted on the surrounding rock.
3 A fragment of clay from the quarry at Skåne is placed on a fine-mesh metal sieve. It will be broken down to reveal any fossil flowers present.
4 The newly discovered fossil from Skåne, freed from its matrix. This is Scandianthus costatus, completely carbonized and stuck to a leaf with resin.

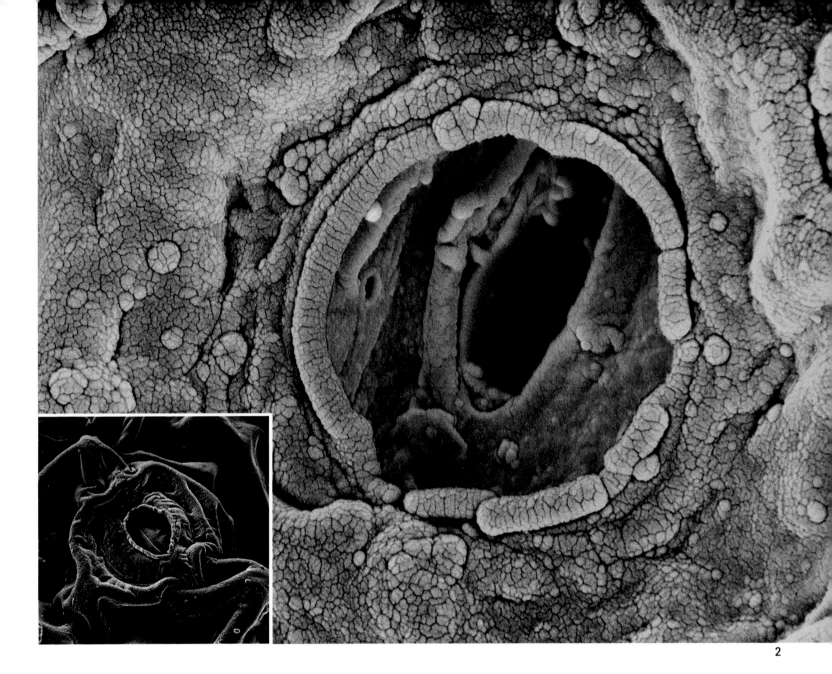

The Evolution of Plants

In the middle of the Palaeozoic Era, towards the end of the Silurian Period – about 400 million years ago – the surface of the earth changed dramatically. The oceans retreated, leaving isolated lakes in low-lying areas. It is thought that the first land plants developed around them. The shrinking of their aquatic environment was probably the major factor in prompting plants to colonize the land, but once they had evolved sufficiently to do so they rapidly spread far and wide.

Before plants were able to manage this astonishing transition, however, certain key developments had to take place. The most important was the evolution of supportive tissue to enable them to stand upright, unsupported by water. Almost as vital was the development of roots and vascular tissue to absorb water and nutrients from the soil and carry them to all parts of the plant. Finally plants required an epidermis, or skin, to reduce water loss and pores to regulate evaporation and the absorption of carbon dioxide from the atmosphere.

The earliest plants to appear on dry land were related to the present-day ferns. One fossil plant, *Scandianthus* (shown here), has been aged at 78 million years, so that it grew towards the end of the Cretaceous Period.

1 *A bud of the fossilized* Scandianthus costatus, *magnified 230 times. The ovary has a ribbed surface covered with small openings, and the tips of the petals can also be seen. This picture was taken under the scanning electron microscope and has been artificially coloured.*
2 *A pore on a* Scandianthus *sepal, magnified 9500 times. The small picture inset on the left shows a pore on a present-day* Vahlia. *The similarity to* Scandianthus *is remarkable. In both plants, the pores are sunk in small hollows surrounded by a circular edge. Extra protection of this kind is often found in evergreens or plants regularly exposed to drought, and also in marsh plants which risk submersion in water.*

2

The Old and the New

There is a remarkable similarity between the two flowers in the picture on the left. To the left of the frame is the fossil *Scandianthus*, and to the right is a dried specimen of a probable living relative, the South African *Vahlia capensis*. A fresh example, from Pretoria in South Africa, is shown above. There is every likelihood that the sepals of the fossil flower were green (the picture has been artificially coloured), but the colour of its petals can only be guessed. Its pot-shaped ovary is visible, together with the stamens, although there are no anthers. The stamens appear to have ripened before the pistil, which happens in the living plants to which *Scandianthus* is probably most closely related. One can also make out the tops of the two styles, complete with stigmas. The fossil flower is only about 2 mm long.

The living South African relative of *Scandianthus* appears to be the nearest modern counterpart to the fossil flower. The ovary, sepals, and petals are visible; the stamens, with the anthers and one pistil, are hidden behind its petals, and only one stigma can be seen. Of eleven features characteristic of *Vahlia*, *Scandianthus* has ten – the most important difference being that the fossil flower has ten stamens in two crowns, whereas *Vahlia* has only one crown of five.

1 *A fossilized* Scandianthus *flower (left) magnified about 80 times, and a dried specimen of the modern South African* Vahlia capensis *(right). The fossil flower has been artificially coloured.*
2 *A fresh example of* Vahlia capensis, *with a beetle on its ovary.*

1

The Fossil Record

The total number of fossils on earth is colossal. One has only to remember that oil consists mainly of fossil animals and coal of fossil plants to get some idea of the quantitites involved. In addition, there are substantial deposits from geological periods both before and after the Carboniferous Era, when oil and coal deposits were formed.

Large parts of the fossil record contain only a limited number of different species, although they occur in great abundance. Some species, on the other hand, are known from only a single specimen. To some extent the frequency of occurrence simply reflects how common or rare a species was in its time, but chance naturally plays a part. Far more fossils remain to be discovered than have come to light already and the great majority of dead plants and animals decompose completely and are never preserved.

Our success in identifying fossil discoveries depends on our now extensive knowledge of the evolutionary relationships among the plant and animal kingdoms. Over the years, researchers have begun to piece together the jigsaw puzzle and today we can be reasonably confident that most of the pieces have been put in their proper place. Most extinct plant species have found their place among earlier finds and their relationship with the flora of today is usually clear.

1 *The stamens of* Vahlia *closely resemble those of* Scandianthus. *In both plants, the anthers are joined to their filaments at the back.*
2 *A section through a* Scandianthus *bud to show its various parts: the green sepal, the yellow petal, the stamens with their filaments and anthers, and two red styles. Colour has been added artificially to make the arrangement clearer.*

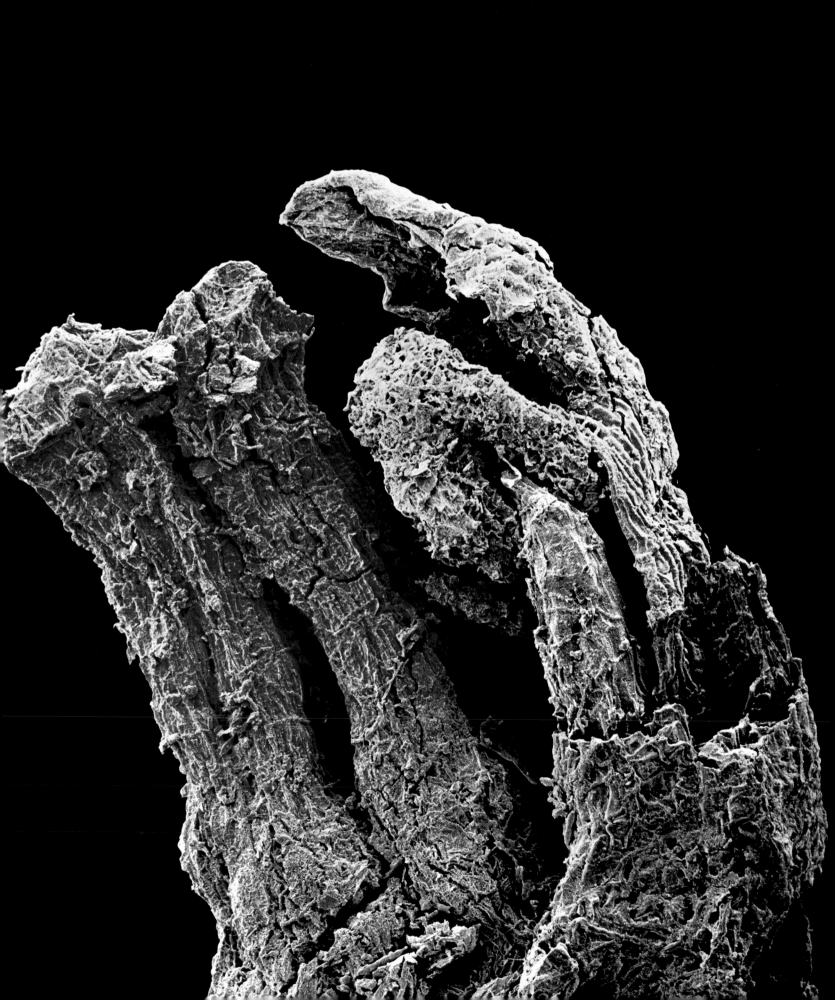

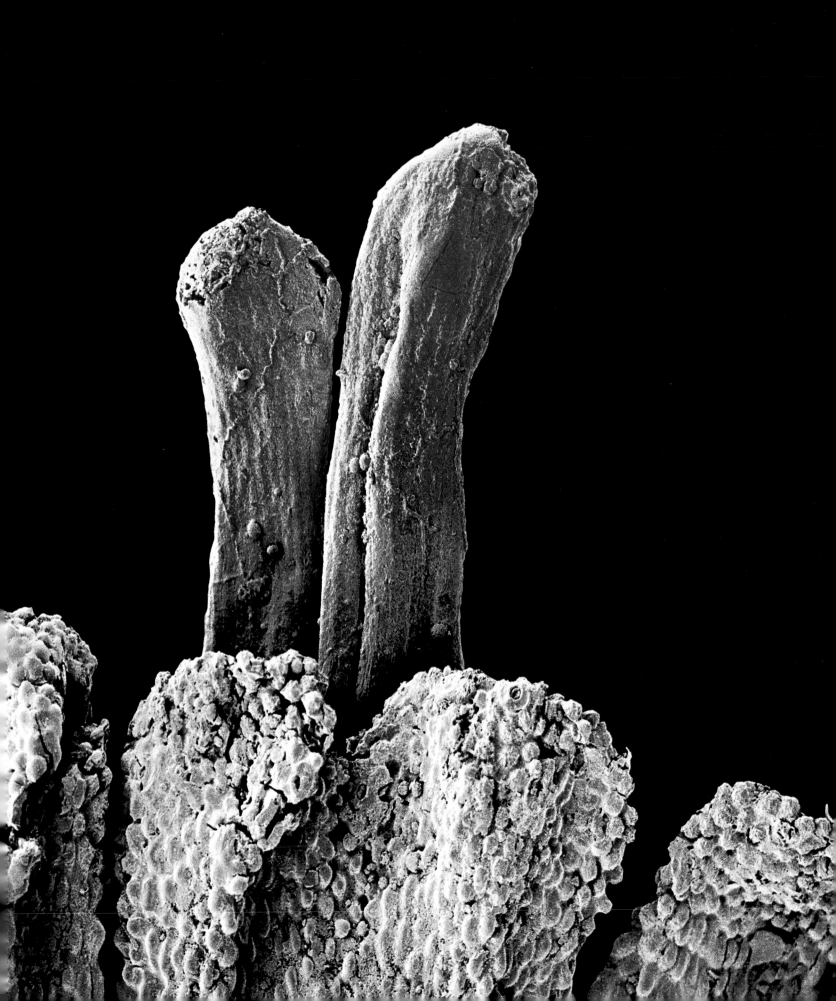

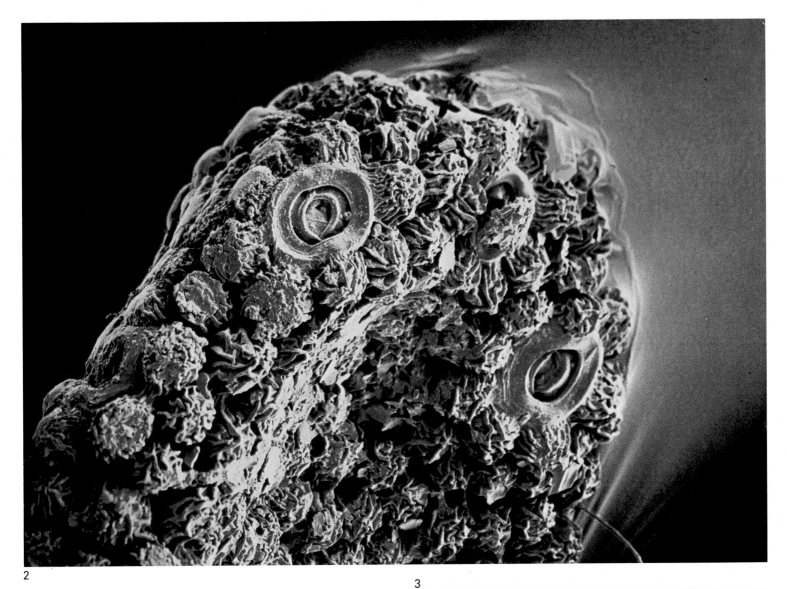

2

Scandianthus

The picture on the opposite page shows the upper part of an ovary of a *Scandianthus* flower. In the centre are two styles and in the foreground two honey-yellow nectaries (colour has been added to make the arrangement clearer). Each *Scandianthus* flower had two double-lobed honey glands positioned in a circle around the two long styles which ran down to the ovary.

   Obviously this species was pollinated by insects, but by what kind we do not know. Bees had not yet evolved when *Scandianthus* was alive; they were not to appear for another thirty million years. The pollinators may have been beetles – a thesis supported by the fact that the present-day *Vahlia* is often visited by them. Associated with the *Scandianthus* finds are the remains of insects which have not yet been identified.

1 *The upper part of a* Scandianthus *ovary.*
2 *Part of the nectaries of a* Scandianthus *flower. The plate-like structures are two pores.*
3 *Part of one of the pores in the previous picture magnified to an even greater degree.*

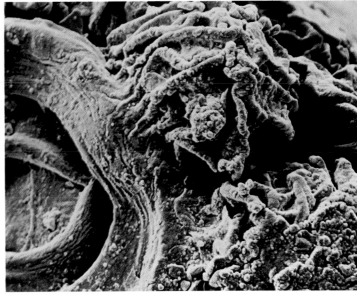

3

Two Ferns

The two germinating ferns on this page are separated by an inconceivable span of time, during which so much has happened in the evolution of life that their remarkable similarity seems quite incredible. A gap of perhaps 350 to 400 million years divides them. When the one on the right germinated, there were neither conifers nor flowering plants; and no higher forms of life such as frogs, reptiles, birds, or mammals. Man would not appear on the scene until less than a quarter of one per cent of the time difference remained.

Yet after hundreds of millions of years, the two plants resemble each other very closely. Perhaps this is because they represent the best solution to the problems that confront all living organisms, even today. No solution, of course, is perfect, for every species changes over time, but undeniably both plants have been able to harmonize their life cycles admirably with the conditions of life on earth.

1 *Another kind of fossil flower from the site where* Scandianthus *was discovered. It is related to the present-day saxifrages, but has not yet been named. Colour has been added artificially.*
2 *A shoot of* Asplenium nidus, *a present-day fern.*
3 *A shoot of a* Spiropteris *fern, checked in its growth some eighty million years ago (colour has been added artificially). The resemblance to* Asplenium nidus *at the same stage of development is remarkable.*

2

3

The Mosquito

A mosquito that lands on your arm is likely to be slapped – if you are quick enough. If not, the mosquito will almost certainly return a few moments later, and this time you may catch it. Why are mosquitoes impelled, apparently suicidally, to bite at all? Since those that do are so often killed, surely other mosquitoes, with less of an appetite for blood, would have a greater chance of survival? Over many generations, therefore, one would expect biting mosquitoes to become rarer and non-biting ones more common. This may sound like a sensible line of reasoning, but in fact it forgets what we know about both Darwinian evolution and the life cycle of the mosquito itself.

Let us start with the mosquito. Its genetic inheritance gives it no choice as to whether to bite or not. A blood-sucking mosquito that never bit anyone would simply starve itself to death. Thus what might appear to be of survival value is in reality only a form of suicide.

If we now look at the problem through Darwinian eyes, we find that since the act of biting is a precondition for the survival of the species, no amount of killing on our part will cause natural selection to favour non-biting rather than biting mosquitoes. Indeed, by killing off the weaker members of the group, we may only make biting mosquitoes more virulent.

Man has, of course, tried time and time again to rid himself of this noxious pest, as well as to eradicate the many other kinds of troublesome insects that can carry disease or damage crops. Every attempt has failed, whether it was pouring toxins into watercourses, where mosquitoes and other insects breed, spraying insecticides, or far more ingenious methods. The insects' invincibility seems to have the strength of a natural law.

The skin of fish is slimy, to reduce friction resistance in the water. The earthworm's muscular body is ideally suited to movement underground. Such adaptations are particularly clear in more extreme living conditions. For example, animals that live as parasites – in or on the bodies of other animals – like the tapeworm, are highly specialized. The mosquito, a carnivore, has evolved a specially shaped mouth in order to perform the demanding and complex task of sucking blood from birds and mammals. In other respects its life cycle resembles those of the majority of the million-odd known species of insect. Indeed, despite the tremendous variety of species and their very different habitats and life styles, all insects are remarkably alike in structure.

All have a tripartite body consisting of head, thorax, and abdomen. On the thorax there are three pairs of legs and on its upper side two folds of skin that have often evolved into wings. On the head there are a pair of compound eyes and usually two antennae, and the whole body is encased in a substance called chitin, which provides an ideal combination of resilience and strength, being both hard and flexible.

There is a very good reason why this huge group should be so similar to one another: they have found a near-perfect solution to the problems of life on earth. The hard chitinous sheath covering the body, combined with their small size, means that insects need little food and air to survive, and water loss is kept to a minimum.

Insects are also able to adapt very quickly to changing conditions and their power of flight allows them to escape danger and even to migrate, should the need arise. They reproduce more quickly and in greater numbers than almost any other kind of life, and so it is hardly surprising that it has proved impossible to eradicate even a single species. They have successfully colonized practically every corner of the earth.

Nearly all insects metamorphose, from egg to larva and then to pupa before the adult insect is hatched. The diet may change at each stage, which eliminates the risk of depending on a single source of food. Finally, a number of species display a degree of social organization almost unparalleled in the animal kingdom – with the exception of man.

In general, mosquitoes share all these advantages. One habitat which forms an important part of their life cycle is human skin, which is why we can expect to be bitten every summer, year after year.

Opposite: a female mosquito can suck its own weight in blood without affecting its ability to fly.

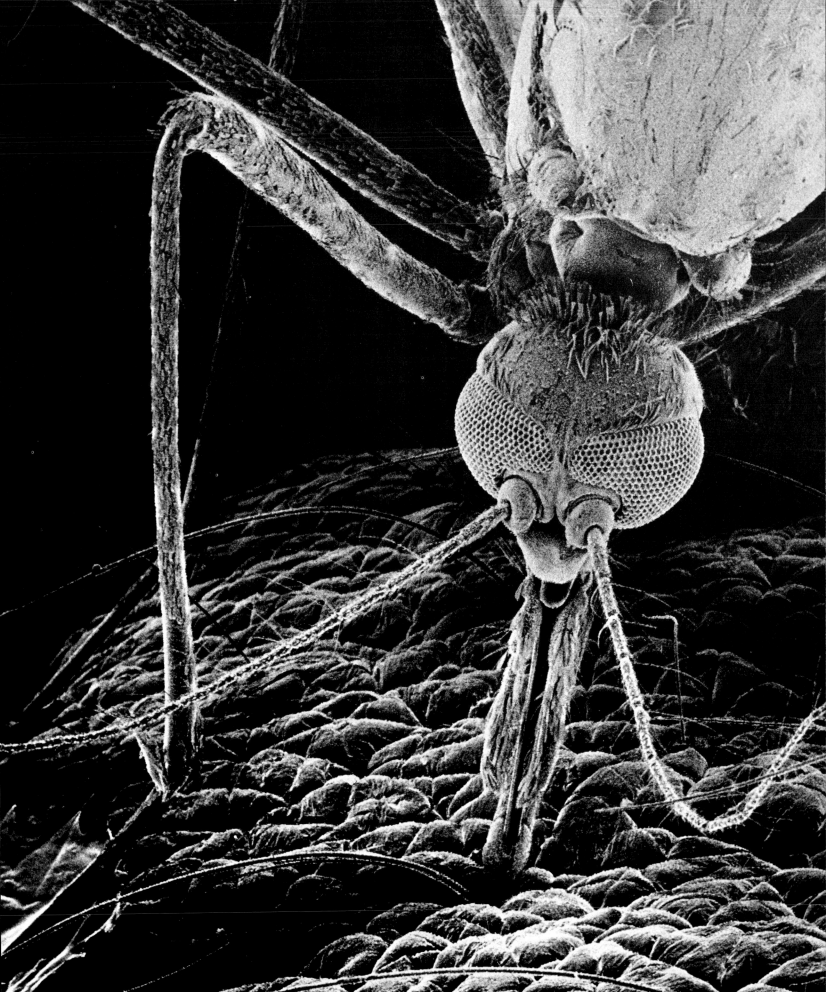

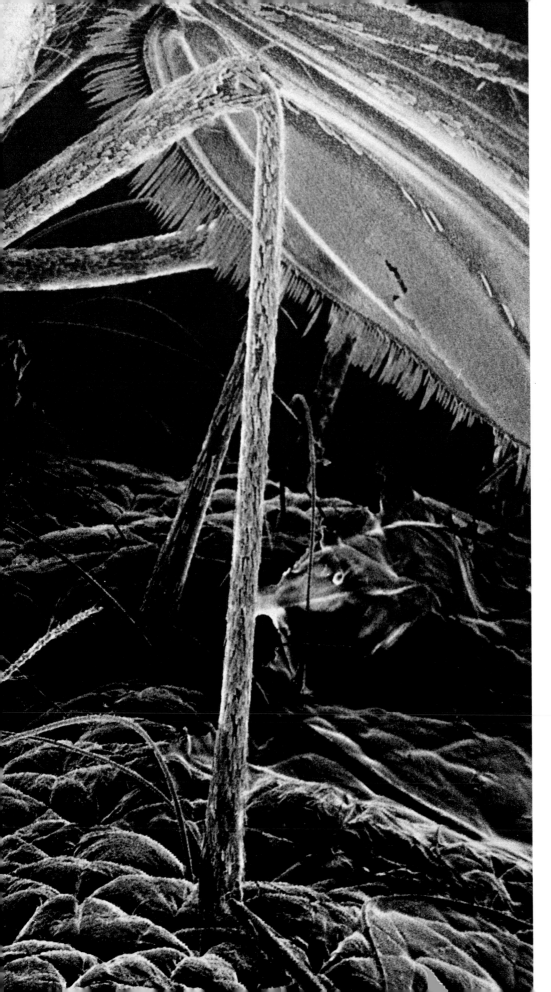

The Mosquito

More than three thousand species of blood-sucking mosquito are known to science. Those that irritate us during the summer mainly belong to just three genera: *Aedes* and *Culex* (the common mosquito) and *Anopheles* (the malarial mosquito).

All mosquitoes are small and delicately built, with graceful limbs, wings, and bodies. They are covered in scales rather than the hairs common to many insects. These form a sheath whose coloration varies from species to species. The malarial mosquito *Anopheles* is easy to distinguish from its relatives because it holds its body at an angle to the surface it has alighted on, whereas the others keep theirs horizontal.

Only the female mosquito bites, needing the proteins in blood to develop her eggs. The males live on nectar and other plant juices. In the far north, where there are few people, the females may also attack other mammals, such as caribou, and birds, particularly young fledgelings in the nest.

Both sexes – separately – form large swarms, the familiar 'clouds' of a summer evening, dancing up and down in the air, often around the tops of trees. Males locate females to mate with by the distinctive sound of their flight, produced by some 600 wing-beats per second.

Mosquitoes transmit not only malaria, but also yellow fever and elephantiasis, among other parasitic infections. After flies, they are the most dangerous of all insects – indeed animals of any kind – to man. Malaria, however, is now confined to the hotter, more southerly parts of the world and in Europe and North America mosquitoes are simply thought of as irritating rather than dangerous. A few hundred years ago the *Anopheles* mosquito did carry a malaria-type disease in Europe, an intermittent fever known as ague, but this seems to have almost died out – we are not sure why – in the early nineteenth century. Today, in areas where malaria has been eradicated or does not occur, this species is as harmless as any other and only its name 'malarial mosquito' reminds us of its former role.

A female Aedes *mosquito sucking blood from human skin. Magnified 45 times under the scanning electron microscope.*

1

2

3

The Bite

Mosquitoes are one of the many insect groups belonging to the order *Diptera*, which literally means two-winged. Their mouth parts are specially designed for biting and sucking. The majority of species have a prominent proboscis formed by a tube-shaped lower lip and elongated upper lip, through which blood and other juices are ingested. There are sensory organs at its base.

When a mosquito bites, a pair of needle-sharp blades on each lip, called stylets, cut through the victim's skin and blood is drawn into the proboscis. At the same time, a special brush-like organ at the tip of the proboscis secretes saliva into the wound. This contains an anti-coagulant and in addition stimulates the flow of blood to the spot. The blood itself is drawn up through a channel formed by the concave inner side of the upper lip and a flat, tongue-like growth (the hypopharynx) in the bottom of the mouth cavity. The mosquito's throat then acts as a suction pump.

Although the females suck blood because they need certain proteins to ensure normal development of their eggs, it is thought that in exceptional cases they can produce healthy eggs without access to blood.

The mosquito itself weighs about five milligrams. It can suck its own weight in blood from a single bite without affecting its ability to fly. The meal takes about four days to digest.

1 *The tip of a mosquito's proboscis. A stylet is protruding from the outer portion of the sheath.*
2 *A stylet in close-up, magnified 340 times. Barb-like spines run along its edges.*
3 *The stylets' sheath, a sensitive 'claw' which feels its way to the exact spot for the bite. The mosquito senses this both chemically and by temperature, finding the right place – between the cell membranes – with great accuracy.*
4 *A female mosquito sucking blood. This specimen is in poor condition, having lost a lot of hairs from its head and body in its search for nourishment.*

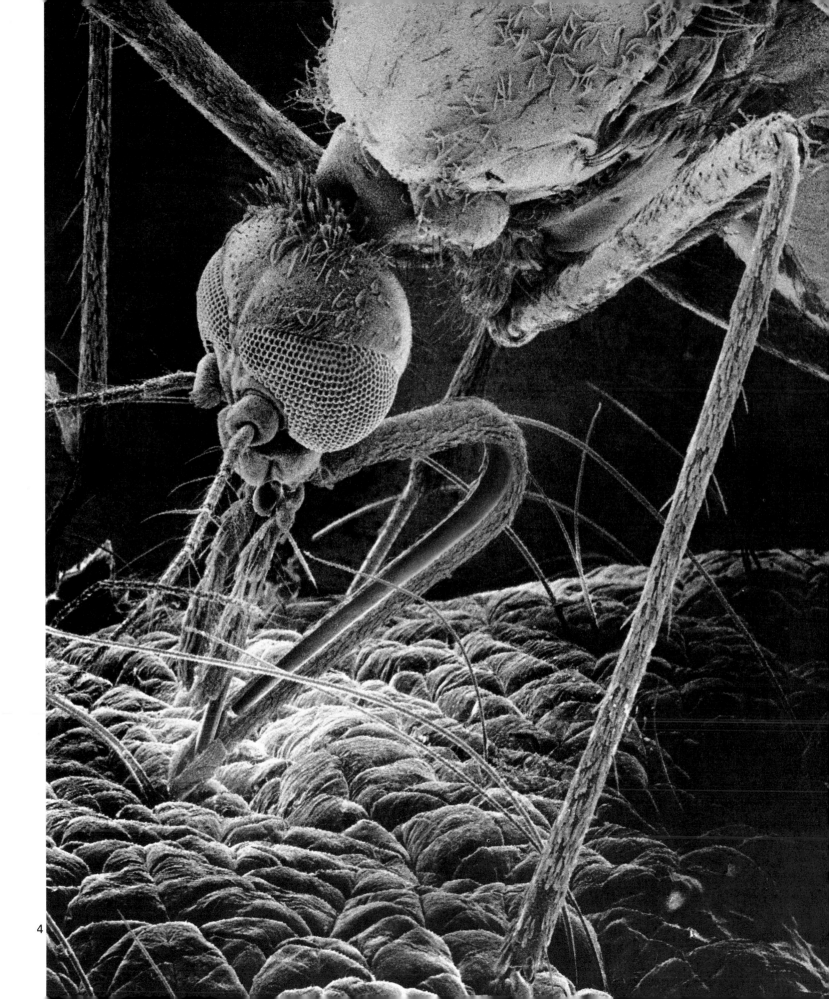

4

1

2

Antennae

Male and female mosquitoes have different antennae. The male's are noticeably hairier and at their base is a special sensor, known as the Johnston organ, which controls the mosquito's sense of balance and hearing. It enables the male to hear the hum of a female's wings, so it can find one to mate with, but filters out the sound of other males. The female's less hairy antennae have no similar organ.

The picture on the opposite page shows something quite extraordinary. The mosquito, tiny enough itself, is carrying a foreign body on its neck. This is a mite, clinging fast to the mosquito's hair. The mite is probably not parasitic on the mosquito, but is simply using it as a means of transport.

1 *The base of the antenna of a male mosquito.*
2 *The base of a female mosquito's antenna.*
3 *A passenger clinging to the hairs on a mosquito's neck: the scanning electron microscope reveals a mite, about 0.05 mm across.*

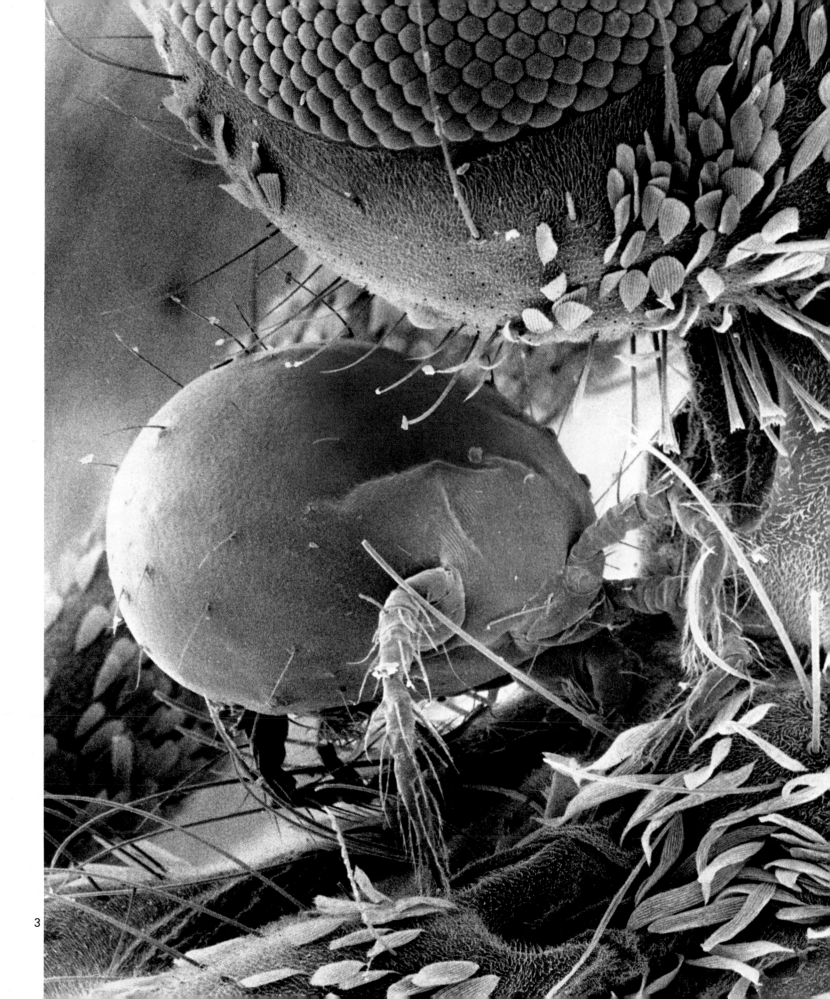

3

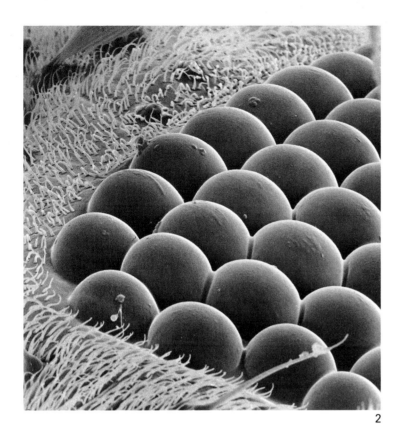

2

3

4

Vision

Mosquitoes have two compound eyes at the front of their head. These are complex in structure and their precise function is not entirely clear. They have no single pupil or lens and no iris, and so cannot focus on an object. Their similarity to the human eye is thus limited; all one can say is that, like our eyes, they serve to register optical phenomena.

The surface of each eye consists of a cornea divided into separate hexagonal segments, or ommatidia, facing outwards. Each individual ommatidium is cone-shaped, with the narrow end pointing inwards, and contains light-sensitive cells. Between these and the cornea there is a transparent cone, perhaps corresponding to the vitreous humour (the clear jelly-like substance that fills the cavity behind the lens) of the vertebrate eye.

A compound eye does not receive a single image, like the human eye, but instead a detailed mosaic of separate images – one from each ommatidium. It seems designed principally to detect movement in the surrounding visual field, in that anything seen to move is displaced from one group of ommatidia to another. The mosquito, therefore, probably does not depend on its primitive vision alone to orientate itself, but uses several sensory functions working together. Quite how this happens is not yet known.

1 *A portrait of a female mosquito, seen obliquely from the front.*
2–4 *Three pictures progressively enlarging the separate elements, or ommatidia, of a mosquito's eye. The first shows a group of ommatidia, the second a single ommatidium magnified about 175 times, and the third shows how the same shapes are repeated in the surface structure of the ommatidium itself. It is covered with tiny peg-like projections which undoubtedly serve some optical purpose, if only by increasing the ommatidium's surface area. The third picture is magnified 28 000 times.*

Touch

An insect's body is encased in the living equivalent of armour – an exoskeleton called a cuticle, which is largely composed of a horn-like substance, chitin. This is like a kind of tough PVC or plastic; it is hard and strong, but at the same time flexible, and is covered with a thin film of wax to restrict water loss. It is not, however, suitable as a base for sensory organs. Instead, most insects are covered with fine bristles or hairs, with a single joint at their base. When the bristle moves, an impulse is transmitted to a nerve cell under the exoskeleton.

Egg-laying

A mosquito can detect the presence of a warm-blooded animal at considerable range. It then homes in by following a combination of smell and body heat. Mosquitoes probably seek out water in which to lay their eggs in the same way.

In order to breed, most mosquitoes prefer stagnant water in lakes or ponds – though water barrels or even empty cans will suffice. The females of *Aedes* and *Culex* lay their eggs tightly together in boat-shaped clumps, but the *Anopheles* mosquito is more choosy, laying its eggs singly and only where the water is clear and clean.

The larvae need access to air in order to breathe and so are invariably found at, or near, the water's surface. They remain there for a few weeks before sinking to the bottom and pupating – the adult hatches after only a few days. Most mosquitoes can produce two broods in a summer, providing there is sufficient water and the temperature is high enough for the eggs to hatch.

Only females survive the winter, spending it in such places as attics and lofts.

1–2 *Scales on a mosquito's neck. They are grouped in a particular area where they act as mechanical receptors, or a kind of sensory organ, by registering the strength of wind resistance. They are directly attached to the cuticle, the insect's outer skin, and are movable on a socket. Around them, actually on the skin, are numerous microscopic hair-like growths whose function is still unknown.*
3–4 *Two other sensory organs, a club-shaped hygro-receptor or moisture-sensitive organs (3), and a chemo-receptor with a pore at its tip (4).*

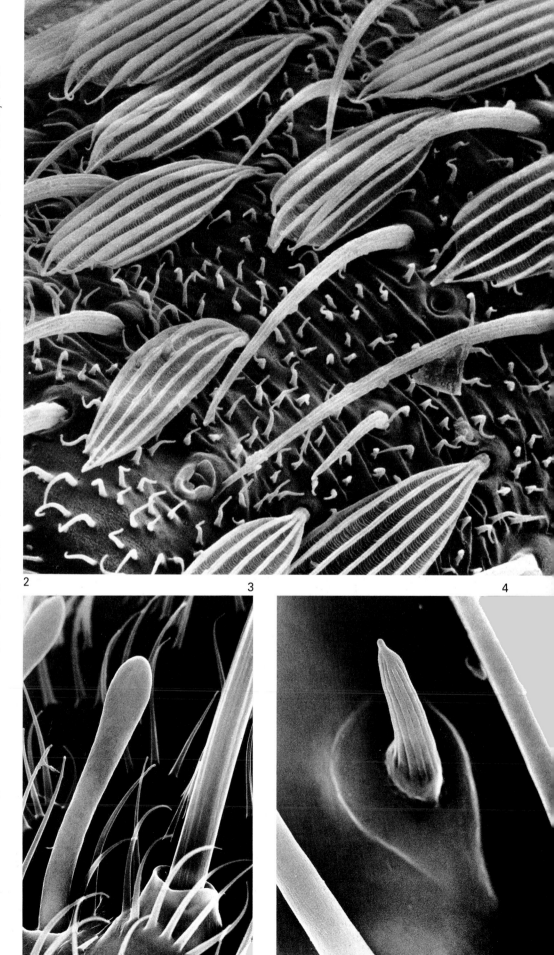

2

3

4

Flight

The great majority of insects have two pairs of wings and use both of them for flight, although in some species the fore-wings have become modified and act simply as covers for the hind-wings. However, mosquitoes belong to the true fliers (the two-winged *Diptera*) and use only their fore-wings for flight. The hind pair, which consist of two small projections called halteres, serve a quite different purpose.

The halteres join the thorax in the same way as fully developed wings, but have only an indirect role during flight. They help to maintain stability or equilibrium. Immediately behind the base joint of the wings, sensory organs detect any deviations in flight from the horizontal plane by monitoring changes in the movement of the halteres. These oscillate up and down at the same speed as the wings.

1 *A haltere, or balancing organ, formed by the mosquito's specially adapted hind-wings.*
2 *The base of a haltere, showing the sensory organ that registers the mosquito's position in relation to the horizontal.*
3 *The sensory organ is composed of layers of cuticle, here magnified about 2200 times.*
4 *One of the world's most successful carnivores: despite its puny size, the mosquito has resisted all efforts to eradicate it.*

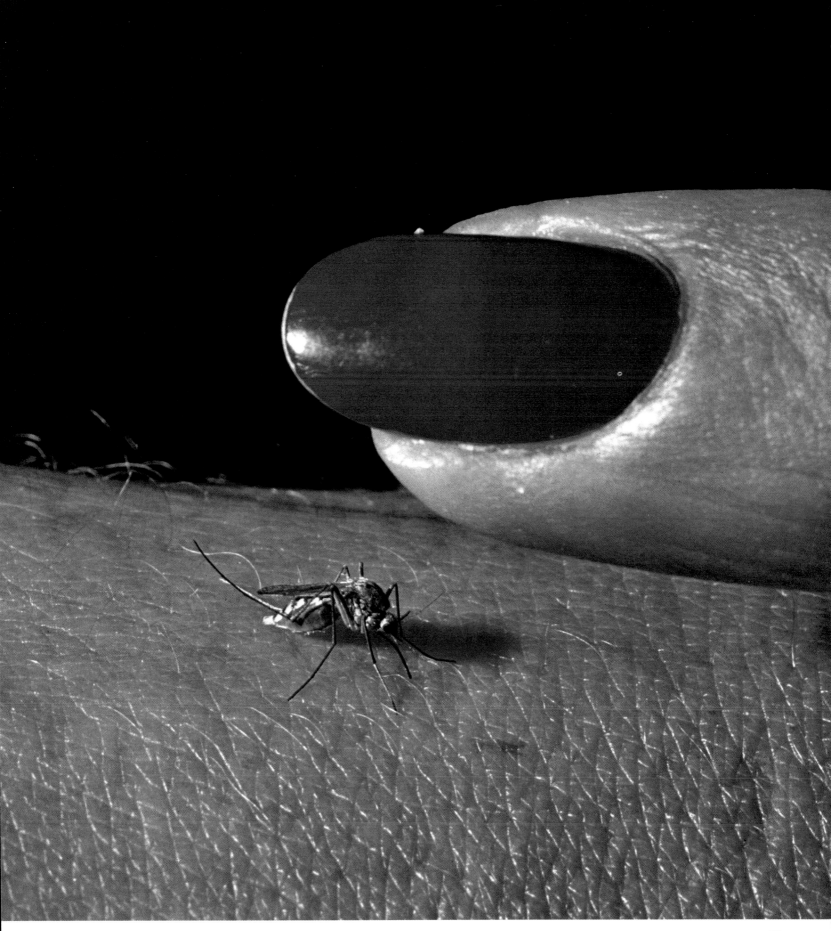

Nature Under the Microscope

Any discussion of what people actually see when they look about them almost always turns to the question of 'selective perception'. We see only what we want to see, and unconsciously close our eyes to everything else. There is undoubtedly a lot of truth in this, but in fact we do not really see what we want to see, we see what we *expect* to see. Someone who knows about the 'halo effect' – the ring of light around the moon on a clear night – is more likely to see it than someone who does not.

However, imagine how exciting it would be if we could learn to see familiar things in an entirely new way. Even the most commonplace object would suddenly take on new meaning. Different degrees of magnification will reveal different things about almost any object, but the aim throughout this book has been to show how objects that normally appear quite unremarkable can become astonishing when seen in another context.

It is often said that the camera can lie by distorting reality. A similar charge can be made against the microscope. But in fact photography can achieve a unique level of realism and truth, and in a sense nature herself has given a lead in optical enlargement. A drop of water can act as a magnifying glass; so can the lens of a fish's eye; and water droplets have existed since the earth first began to cool.

The art of making lenses was known in antiquity, and when the first microscopes were developed three hundred years ago they did little more than extend a well-known principle. The modern microscope, with its double-lens system and light to illuminate the object to be studied, is a further refinement. However, conventional microscopes are limited by the laws of optics to a maximum magnification of about 2000 times. Beyond this objects simply become bigger, not clearer.

The electron microscope, which was invented about fifty years ago, allows almost unlimited magnification. An object less than a millionth of a millimetre in size can be given sharp definition. The instrument works by using electromagnetic (rather than glass) lenses to focus beams of electrons onto an object. The beams are then projected onto a fluorescent screen or photographic plate. Because the wavelength of an electron beam is 120000 times shorter than that of light, it is able to 'reflect' an object with very much greater resolution.

But any tool is only as good as the person who uses it. To photograph the hidden world of nature requires care, skill, and experience. An object must be shown as accurately as possible, and with an artist's eye for its composition and form. In nature the gap between art and science is not always unbridgeable. Water drops can act as lenses, and lenses of another kind can be found on the leaves of certain plants. Their precise function is still unknown, but they often occur on tropical plants – on tradescantias, for example, as shown here. It is possible that these living lenses may have evolved as a response to the gloom of the forest floor, by concentrating the amount of light available to the cells of the leaf.

1

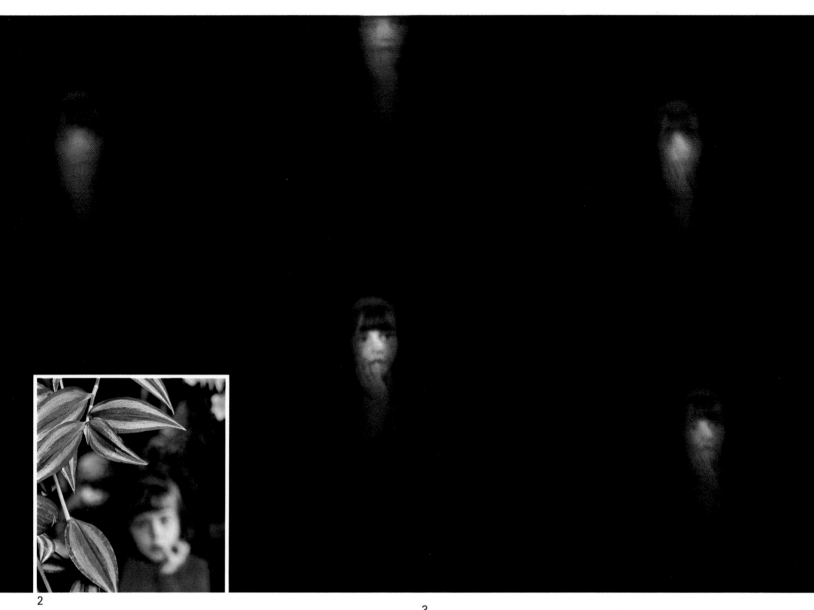

1 *A leaf of a tradescantia, commonly called the wandering Jew. With the aid of a magnifying glass one can see that the surface is covered with small, wart-like lenses.*

2 *In the inset picture above a little girl sits close to a tradescantia plant. In the bigger picture (magnified about 2000 times) the girl's image appears in the 'lenses' on the surface of the leaf. The image is projected directly onto the surface of the leaf via a mirror placed under the microscope – there is no other lens between the girl and the leaf.*

3 *Lennart Nilsson (foreground) and researcher Berndt Ödarp at work on the electron microscope. They are photographing a mosquito for this book.*